THE COMPLETE GUIDE

BUYING AND SELLING REAL ESTATE

THE COMPLETE GUIDE TO
BUYING AND SELLING REAL ESTATE

Making the Most of the American Dream

LOWELL R. HODGKINS

BETTERWAY PUBLICATIONS, INC.
WHITE HALL, VIRGINIA

Published by Betterway Publications, Inc.
Box 219
Crozet, VA 22932

Cover design and photograph by Susan Riley
Typography by East Coast Typography

Library of Congress Cataloging-in-Publication Data

Hodgkins, Lowell R.
  The complete guide to buying and selling real estate: making the most of the American dream / Lowell R. Hodgkins.

    p.   cm.
  Includes index.
  ISBN: 1-55870-118-4 : $9.95
  1. House buying. 2. House selling. 3. Real property. 4. Real estate
business.   I. Title.
HD1379.H58   1989   88-37711
333.33′0973—dc19   CIP

Printed in the United States of America
098765432

To Maria —
thanks for your patience and support.

Acknowledgments

I wish to acknowledge the California Association of Realtors, the Regional Data Service, the Menlo Park-Atherton Board of Realtors, and Fellowes Realty for their cooperation and permission to use the forms reproduced in this book.

Preface

INTENDED AUDIENCE

For most Americans, the purchase of their home ranks as one of the really great thrills of their lives. It can also be one of the most frightening ventures that they have ever undertaken. For some, this will be the only home that they will ever own; but for many more in this land of high mobility, this process will be repeated a number of times during the course of their lives.

Each year, millions of homes change ownership, and for each and every one of these transactions there obviously has to be at least one buyer and one seller. The vast majority of these buyers and sellers are not knowledgeable experts in the field of real estate. Furthermore, they are more than likely buying or selling the greatest asset that they will ever own. It is, therefore, quite understandable that a large majority of these transactions are accompanied by a great deal of fear and emotion.

It is to each and every person contemplating, either now or in the future, the purchase or sale of residential real property that this book is dedicated.

GOALS OF THE BOOK

The intended goal, quite simply, is to replace fear and uncertainty with knowledge and confidence. For the buyer, this means knowing that he is making the best possible purchase, given the constraints of his or her personal financial capabilities and the local market conditions. For the seller, it usually means feeling confident that he is receiving the best possible price and terms, given what he considers a reasonable time to properly market the property.

Knowledge breeds confidence. In order to develop confidence, it is necessary to broaden one's knowledge and understanding of the subject at hand. In the case of residential real estate transactions, this requires developing an understanding of the legal and financial complexities of the transaction, acquiring the ability to measure the economic worth of the property, and learning how to cut through all of the underlying emotions that are so very often involved.

This book will provide all of the tools and insight required to do this and much more.

Contents

Introduction to Residential Real Estate

REAL ESTATE IS REAL ESTATE, BUT —

Home ownership has been the Great American Dream for millions upon millions of Americans. Nowhere else on earth does such a large proportion of the population enjoy the benefits of owning one's own home. Pride of ownership is exemplified in one manicured neighborhood after another across the breadth and depth of this great country.

But for most Americans, home ownership represents much more than just the pride, the sovereignty, and the safe haven; it also represents the best investment and the greatest asset that they own. For so many, no other investment begins to compare to the appreciation that they have realized over the years as the result of owning their own home. The degree to which this is true, however, depends upon when and where the home was purchased.

Homes purchased in the early 1970's in much of San Mateo County (south of San Francisco) for about $35,000 were selling from $275,000 to well over $300,000 in 1987. At the same time, homes purchased in Boise, Idaho in 1981 were worth less in 1987. The value of homes in southern New Jersey (suburban Philadelphia) remained relatively flat for a number of years while other areas around the country were appreciating at fairly rapid rates, but have appreciated smartly during the last few years.

A home came on the market during the summer of 1986 in Atherton, California for $549,000. It was a nice home and was well-priced for Atherton, but because it was on the corner of a residential but none-the-less busy through street, it took over six months to sell. If the home had been one block removed, it would have sold within weeks at that price. There, the difference of a block or two can have an effect of as much as $100,000 on the value of a given property. On the other hand, if this same home were situated in, say, Fulton, New York, it might not be worth more than $75,000 to $100,000.

It is easy to see that although residential real estate in general has been a good investment over the past thirty years or so, it has provided a much better investment for some than others, strictly as a result of timing and location.

It is felt by many that the opportunity for unusually large appreciations in homes has now passed. In areas of severe economic depression, such as Houston and Boise, home values have actually decreased dramatically. However, given a reasonably healthy economic climate, it is a sure bet that home values will at least keep pace with inflation, and in a great many locations, they will appreciate more rapidly and somewhat independently from overall inflation, primarily because of supply and demand influences.

THE 1986 TAX LAW

The 1986 federal income tax overhaul was signed into law over two years ago and will be fully implemented in 1989. These new regulations will have an adverse effect on the value of income producing properties as an investment in the future. Such investments will no longer be the safe havens from the heavy hand of the IRS that they used to be. Simply stated, such investments will have to make sense before taxes rather than after taxes. This is a subject well beyond the scope of this book.

What should not be overlooked, and the reason for bringing this subject up, however, is that the tax law still favors home ownership. It should be further noted that this includes not only your first home, but also a second, or vacation, home as well Mortgage interest and local real estate taxes on these properties are still fully deductible.

As a result of this new legislation, income property will have to stand on its own merits as an investment without tax considerations. This will make many properties very unattractive as an investment as they are currently structured. For them to become attractive in the future, the cost vs. income ratio will have to decrease.

In the case of apartments, this could well mean severe increases in rents over the next few years. As this happens, another segment of society will find that it no longer makes economic sense to rent rather than own.

This will add to the demand for affordable housing at the same time that investors will either "want out" of their income property investments or cer-

tainly have no interest in investing in such properties under current cost vs. income ratios. This could easily result in a vicious cycle that will continue to inflate the value of residential real estate.

The bottom line, then, is that while income producing real estate at its present cost vs. income ratio will become a less attractive investment, home ownership (both first and second) will continue to be one of the best investments the average family can make.

This is true as things now stand; however, most experts feel that Congress will continue to make revisions in tax legislation. It should come as no surprise if most of what was implemented in the 1986 legislation changes again in the next several years.

SOME PROBLEM AREAS

There are two major problem areas that have existed regardless of the tax overhaul, and that could well be intensified as a result of it.

The first of these problems is the increasing difficulty for the average young couple to come up with a sufficient down payment and/or to be able to qualify for a mortgage as the cost of housing rises faster than incomes. Some creative ideas that will successfully address this problem should result from the inevitable real estate shakeup that will take place over the next several years.

The second major problem facing our society lies in providing proper housing for our rapidly increasing population of senior citizens. This market is being studied carefully by a number of major corporations, but again, some truly innovative thinking is going to be necessary to solve the growing needs in this area.

These problem areas are each major subjects on their own; the second problem, the future plight of our senior citizens, is a social concern of enormous proportions. However, the first problem, that of the entry-level purchaser, strikes at the very core of what this book is all about, the ability of the largest possible segment of our population to enjoy home ownership.

WINNERS AND LOSERS

In all financial transactions, there is always the possibility that the transaction will result in a winner and a loser. This is certainly true in the buying and selling of residential real estate. Although I feel that most residential real estate transactions can and should result in a win-win situation, the purpose of this book is to provide sufficient knowledge and insight so that its readers, at the very least, will never be losers in such a transaction.

PREVIEW OF COMING ATTRACTIONS

Beyond this introduction, this book is divided into two parts.

The first part is devoted to the needs of the buyer. As we march step-by-step through the entire process of purchasing a home, we will explore the emotions as well as the economics of the purchase process. Much will be discussed concerning the intricacies of financing and the various legal ramifications. The subject of title will be investigated. Sample forms will be utilized and referred to throughout. With knowledge and understanding each and every reader approaching the marketplace can be a well-informed, sophisticated buyer.

Part two is devoted to the needs of the seller. Often, selling one's home can be an agonizing and traumatic experience, full of memories, some fond, some sad. This can present a real problem, because emotions don't help when contemplating the sale of a major asset. Potential sellers should be as objective as possible when approaching the marketplace.

We will explore in depth the financial and legal aspects of selling one's home. Determining the highest realistic price is of prime importance. Understanding listing agreements, purchase contracts, offers, counter-offers, the impact and removal of contingencies, and seller involvement in financing — all are necessary.

Everyone who has been through the agonies of selling a home will tell you that it is just not fun. Trying to keep the home in show-perfect condition practically twenty-four hours a day, vacating for Sunday open houses, worrying and wondering if and when the house will ever sell — all add up to a serious disruption of lifestyle, frequent invasions of privacy, and considerable mental anguish.

Although I doubt seriously that I can make selling your home a fun experience in your life, my aim is to cut the agony to a minimum by telling you how to get the job done quickly and efficiently, with the confidence that accompanies superior knowledge of the subject at hand.

THE NECESSARY AGENT

No matter how knowledgeable you may become as the result of this or any other study material that might be available, the chances are that you will end up buying or selling through a licensed real estate agent. Choosing the right agent (and you do have a choice) may well be the most important real estate decision you will ever make.

Although more will be said about the buyer-agent and the seller-agent relationships later, some general things about agents come to mind. Picture an agent; agents come in a wide variety of sizes, shapes, colors, and nationalities. Some are male and some are female. There are greenhorns and there are old salts. There are full-timers and there are part-timers. There are professionals and there are amateurs.

What you should be looking for, first and foremost, is an honest and knowledgeable individual, working full time and representing a solid and reputable real estate agency, who will treat your best interests as paramount. The question is, where do you find and how do you recognize this rare gem.

It may not be too easy. Less than 10% of all licensees are still in business five years after first becoming licensed. The vast majority are gone within the first two years. It would seem reasonable and prudent not to want to get involved with the 90+% who will be disappearing into the woodwork in the not-too-distant future.

This is not to say, however, that a relatively new agent cannot do an excellent job for you. Every year new stars are born all across the country in this business. There is an age-old saying in the real estate business: 80% of the business is handled by only 20% of the agents. This was true nearly thirty years ago when I first became licensed as a real estate agent, and it is just as true today — maybe even more so.

There are many areas of the country where there are literally more licensed agents than there are transactions in an entire year. It is obvious, then, that the vast majority of the agents are not making any money at all from the business, while the relatively few stars are making a very good living indeed. It should be well noted, however, that I have never met a high income agent who did not work hard and earn every single dollar that came his or her way.

From your point of view as the potential buyer or seller, it should be irrelevant how much money your agent earns. However, an agent's financial success is generally an indication of his or her professionalism and dedication to the business.

On the other hand, very often a successful agent gets so busy that he cannot give his best effort to all his clients at the same time. The really smart ones know when they are approaching this situation and begin backing off. However, sometimes an agent is so popular that this is not possible.

Popular or not, if the agent does not do something to relieve the strain, his popularity will diminish rapidly when he fails to service his clients properly.

An excellent solution to such a situation is for the busy agent to bring in an assistant to help with the legwork. This would generally be a new agent who has not yet developed the clientele to keep him busy. They will work out an appropriate commission split between themselves, and two purposes are satisfied at one time. The clients' needs are satisfied without a compromise in capabilities and the new agent gets valuable training.

So how do you recognize the right agent for you? First, do not judge an agent's success solely by the clothes he wears or the car he drives. I know several new agents who went out and purchased new BMWs and Mercedes as prerequisites to entering the real estate business. The question is still very much unanswered as to how successful most of these individuals will ever be.

Instead, look first for competence. By the time you finish reading this book, you should be able to recognize incompetence very quickly. There is no immediate cure for incompetence — disassociate yourself from the incompetent agent immediately!

Next, you want honesty. Again, your knowledge as a result of reading this book will help you detect when an agent is not being straight with you. There will be times when you know something is wrong, but you cannot make up your mind whether the person is being deceitful or is just plain incompetent. Who cares? Just get away fast.

Finally, you want empathy. If someone is going to take on the job of being your agent in either the purchase or sale of possibly your greatest asset, you want that person to be sincerely concerned about your needs and desires. To do this, an agent has to get to know a lot about you — get into your head, so to speak. If you are a very private person, this may be difficult for you to allow. However, your agent needs a lot of information in order to serve you best. This involves a knowledge and understanding of your present lifestyle and financial capabilities, as well as your dreams and aspirations for the future and realistic long-term income projections.

If you are convinced that your agent is knowledgeable and competent, it should not take very long to sense whether he has your best interests at heart.

There are plenty of competent agents out there who are simply more interested in making the sale or getting the listing than in serving the best interests of the client. These people are even reasonably honest, but their priorities are mixed up. They are thinking commissions first, client's best interest second.

There are still others who are so wrapped up in their own egos, there is simply no room to empathize with the needs of others. These agents will never have a clue as to their clients' true needs and desires.

A reasonably perceptive person generally has a very good ability to sense whether or not someone is conducting himself with his or her best interest at heart. If you feel comfortable, stick with it. If not, make a change.

Whatever you do, do not ever let any agent coerce you into believing that you are either legally or morally obligated to do business through him or her when you would prefer to do otherwise. This does not mean that you can or should use an agent to your advantage and then simply discard this person when you feel you do not need anything more. The Golden Rule is a two-way street. It also

does not mean that you can simply negate your legal contractual obligations for no good reason.

What it does mean, however, is that simply because you have been thrown together with an agent by chance, say by calling and inquiring about a property for sale or stopping by an open house, that agent does not own you forevermore as a client. A lot of agents think like this and become downright possessive. The point is, if you are not comfortable doing business with a particular agent, and you have not gone so far that you are now contractually obligated to continue, then you don't have to! That's the law!

Finally, now that we have explored all that you can and should expect from your agent, let's take a look at what the agent has a right to expect from you.

Honesty? You bet. Loyalty? Up to a point. As long as the agent is working for you and you are satisfied, be loyal. If, on the other hand, you are not satisfied and you don't think things are going that well, then say so. Maybe things can be done differently. If that does not work or you have simply reached the point where you do not want to carry on any further, then break it off and go out and establish a new relationship. But be honest. Tell him what is on your mind and what you are planning. You may have to be firm because he may try to dissuade you, but this way, by being straight and up front, you can part in a civilized manner and you can feel comfortable with your role in the entire relationship.

Remember, you are the boss. But also remember the Golden Rule.

Part 1
Purchasing Your Dream

1
Getting Psyched Up

Spending Sunday afternoons visiting open houses that are for sale is a favorite pastime of many Americans. They are really not in the market, so they tell themselves; it's just kind of fun to look and dream.

Well, let me tell you, every week some little percentage of these folks who were "just looking" end up buying. Is this impulse buying, or was visiting open houses just their unconscious way of getting psyched up to make the big plunge?

Whatever the case, it is important to get psyched up to the idea of buying a home, whether it is a first-time purchase or a move up. Naturally, there are economic realities which we will get into shortly; but first and foremost, the prospect of buying a new home should be exciting, and the search for that dream home should be fun.

Home ownership is not for everyone, but if you are reading this book, it is probably something that you have at least considered as being desirable. It is my opinion that home ownership is the single most important element in the myriad of things that make up the notion of quality of life.

No matter how humble or how grand the home may be, the pride of ownership, the "safe haven"

feeling of security, and the family cohesiveness that is a part of home ownership are irreplaceable once you have experienced them.

In this day and age there is a wide variety of ownership possibilities to consider. If you are just getting started and cannot afford too much, then a small condo with a low down payment requirement may be your best bet. If you hate commuting, then a house or condo near your place of employment is probably your best answer. If you have school age children, then a home with lots of room and a nice yard in a good school district is a desirable goal. If you hate gardening and maintenance, then the condo or townhouse is a worthwhile consideration. If you love gardening, then maybe it's a move toward the country and a little more land to tend. If your family has grown and moved on, then it may be time to find something smaller and easier to care for. As you can see, the reasons for buying a new home are virtually endless, and as individual as the people involved. Whatever your reasons may be, the best way to get psyched up and stay psyched up long after the deed has been done, is to plan carefully each and every move you'll make. Without such a plan, you will find yourself flailing about with serious financial doubts, agonizing over what to do, moving back and forth between highs of excitement and depths of depression and anxiety. This is definitely not fun.

Once you work out a plan with the help of this book, the fun can begin. With the self-assurance that comes with knowing that you are making a good economic decision, then you can really go out and thoroughly enjoy the search for that dream home.

THREE CRITERIA TO BE SATISFIED

Any home purchase, whether it is your very first home or your second or your fifteenth, should satisfy three basic criteria in order to be considered a proper purchase.

First, you should like it. It should fulfill your present needs. It may not be the ultimate of everything that you desire, but it should be a definite improvement over whatever you will be moving away from, and if it is not the ultimate, then it should be considered a major stepping stone toward that ultimate. But in the meantime, you should truly be able to look forward with a reasonable amount of excitement and expectation to the joys of your new home. If you really cannot muster up such feelings, then you should reconsider the decision to purchase.

Next, you should be able to afford it. This is an area that we will explore in depth in the next section. Suffice it to say here that if you can't afford it, you are going to learn to hate it. That is definitely not what home ownership is all about.

Finally, the purchase of your home should be a good investment. At the very least, it should keep up with inflation. At best, it could appreciate at rates well above the national or even local inflation rates.

It should be remembered, however, that almost all geographic areas have economic fluctuations, and there are better times then others to buy. Earlier, we talked about the tremendous appreciation experienced by folks who bought in the San Francisco bay area in the early 1970's. However, some purchases that were made in 1980 and 1981 in the very same area turned out to be losers when they had to be sold just a year or two later. The market reached its zenith in 1980, and then corrected slightly over the next two years. During that short time interval, those who bought at the peak and then turned around and sold shortly thereafter lost money after sales expenses were paid.

Had those same people waited until 1985 or 1986 to sell, they would have had no problem in realizing an appreciation that would have rivaled any other reasonably low risk investment that they might have made at that time.

There are many things that can affect the value of a home. However, no matter what the precipitating cause, it always boils down to the basics of supply and demand. Today, the housing market is a shambles in Houston, Texas. Why? Oil prices, you say. True, but let's examine what that has meant. Lower prices have resulted in massive layoffs in oil-related industries. People have to eat, and they cannot feed their families if there is no money coming in. So if they cannot find work in Houston, then they must go elsewhere. Result? A very large supply and a very small demand for houses in Houston. The values have taken a nose dive. Right now the very best buys in the country are in Houston, Texas for anyone who can afford to hold on and wait for the Houston economy to turn around. And it will turn around.

An extremely high interest rate was the culprit in the early 1980's. With interest rates as high as 15-18%, no one was about to move unless they absolutely had to, or they simply did not understand the economics of the times. Since new construction is generally planned years in advance, it does not immediately turn off the minute interest rates suddenly rise. This was true in the early 1980's. So housing units were being erected for a time when there was little or no demand. As mentioned earlier, property values which peaked in 1980 corrected during the next several years due to this temporary change in the relationship of supply to demand.

Normally, we would think of such a situation, where the supply is increasing at the same time that demand is declining, as a buyer's market. However, in this case, with interest rates so high, the only buyers to profit from the situation were those with all cash who did not have to concern themselves about interest rates.

As you contemplate the purchase of a home, you must consider the economic strength of the nation in general and of your local area in particular.

During the great Depression of the 1930's, very few could afford a home, and the values were very low. Imagine the buys you could have made if only you had the money. That is precisely when and how some of our wealthiest families made their fortunes. We are probably fairly well protected against another great depression, but we have had and will undoubtedly continue to have major recessions from time to time. During these periods one should expect that values might decrease, however, in recent years we have experienced the phenomena of recession and inflation at the same time, which tends to boggle even the best of economic minds.

Generally speaking, however, the best time to buy should be near the end of a recessionary cycle. There are basically two things wrong with this for the average home buyer. First, he does not have a crystal ball and hence has no way of knowing precisely when this is going to occur. But even more important, he wants to buy when he wants to buy, regardless of economic cycles.

The best advice I know is this: Try to ascertain that your local economy is not riding an artificial high that really has no sound economic reason for being, and might burst and descend at any moment. This could happen if a major employer in the area were to shut down.

Pick a neighborhood that is not experiencing or about to experience economic obsolescence, some major change that will cause it to lose value as a whole. This could be caused by the impending construction of a major highway in close proximity that will change the entire character of the neighborhood, and not for the better. It could also be caused by a change in zoning or in the socio-economic mix in a neighborhood.

Of crucial importance, be sure that you are not paying over fair market value for your home. Here is where emotion can get in the way to your great disadvantage. No matter how much you are in love with it, you cannot afford to overpay if you want it to become a worthwhile investment. Shop smart. Ask your agent to provide comparables before you sign a contract. These comparables of recently sold properties are readily available through most multiple listing services, and allow you to pinpoint exactly what people have been paying for similar properties. If you cannot get your hands on this vital information, then you are either trying to go it alone or you are dealing with the wrong agent.

Finally, do not buy a property that is an over-improvement for the neighborhood. If it is a neighborhood of $90,000 homes, do not buy one for $125,000, even if it is by far the grandest home in the area. The economic law of regression dictates that the average value of a neighborhood tends to pull down the value of the most expensive homes in that neighborhood, particularly if they are obvious over-improvements for that neighborhood.

If you follow all of the advice to this point, the chances of your home becoming one of the best investments that you will ever make are exceedingly good.

CONFRONTING THE ECONOMIC REALITIES

For the average home buyer, there are two areas of financial concern: how much down and how much per month?

First, let's consider the down payment and all other initial cash requirements necessary to make the purchase. Down payments can be as low as zero, depending upon how creative the financing is, or up to 25% or more, depending upon the property and the type and availability of desired mortgage financing.

In addition to the actual cash down payment which is applied toward the purchase price and placed in escrow on or before the date of closing, there are significant one time cash requirements which will also have to be satisfied at the time of closing. These are called closing costs and we will get into them in great detail later in the book. For the purposes of this section, we will break the closing costs into two broad categories: the loan origination fee and all other closing costs.

The loan origination fee, better known as "points," is the amount of money the lender charges up front to make the loan. It is usually stated as a percentage of the amount of the loan. At the present time, loan origination fees range from 1-2%; however, during times of tight money and especially in funding FHA and VA loans when their rates are non-competitive, these loan origination fees have soared to as much as 10-15%. These fees are withheld as a part of the closing fees.

The balance of the closing fees covers a myriad of charges which include title insurance, pro-ration of taxes and assessments, prepayment of taxes and insurance, payment of notary and recording fees, the payment of any other expenses accrued in conjunction with the purchase, and the fee charged by the escrow company for performing these services. For estimating purposes, you can generally figure on 1-1.25% of the sale price for these miscellaneous costs.

In order to fully understand this very important aspect, consider the following example. Let's say that you buy a home for $100,000.00 and decide to pay 20% down and finance the balance with a loan that will have a 1.5% loan origination fee. The following is a reasonable estimate of what your up front cash requirements will be:

Down Payment (20% of $100,000)	$20,000.00
Loan Origination Fee (1.5% of $80,000)	$ 1,200.00
Balance of Closing Costs (1.25% of $100,000)	$ 1,250.00
Total Estimated Cash Requirements	$22,450.00

It's quite obvious that before you consider the purchase of a home, you must first ascertain how much cash you can comfortably come up with to put into that purchase. Once you have made this determination, recognizing that a portion of this will have to be used for closing costs, then the next step is to determine how large a mortgage you can comfortably afford to carry.

Most banks analyze this problem based upon the ability to repay the indebtedness. To do this, they look at the borrower's indebtedness as a percentage of his gross income (before taxes are deducted). Different banks use different criteria, but the norm is referred to as 33/38. This means that they expect that monthly housing expenses which include principal, interest, taxes, and insurance will not exceed 33%. Furthermore, they also expect that total long term indebtedness (anything with amortized payments such as car loans that stretch over one year), including housing expenses, will not exceed 38% of gross income.

Let's consider an example. Our potential borrower in this example is a married couple with a combined family gross income of $58,000. They have an auto loan that has over two years to go with monthly payments of $192.00 per month, and an education loan that they will be paying for another three years at the rate of $125.00 per month.

Thirty-three percent of $58,000 = $19,140 divided by 12 = $1,595.00 per month which can be applied to housing expenses. A loan in the amount of $160,000 at 9.5% fixed interest, amortized over thirty years, would have a monthly payment of $1,345.37.

Taxes vary widely from community to community. In California, since the enactment of Proposition 13, taxes are essentially 1% of the purchase price. Let's assume a purchase price of $178,000. Taxes would amount to $1,780.00 divided by 12 = $148.33 per month. Insurance should cost about $70.00 per month.

Total housing expenses in this example, including principal, interest, taxes, and insurance, will run $1,563.70 per month, just under the 33% guideline of $1,595.00.

However, when the bank looks at the long term total indebtedness payments of $192.00 for the auto and $125.00 for the education loan added to the $1563.70 for housing expenses, the total of $1,880.70 turns out to be slightly over the 38% guideline for total long term indebtedness, which calculates out to $1,836.67.

In this example, I would expect that the bank would have no problem approving the loan. The 33/38 percentages are meant to be guidelines, and other extenuating circumstances are taken into consideration. Individuals or families with obvious upward mobility in their future earnings potential will often be approved with somewhat higher debt-to-earnings ratios than the 33/38 guidelines. On the other hand, someone with a blemished credit record might well expect a bank to adhere very strictly to the guidelines, if they are willing to make the loan at all.

Now you have an insight as to what a bank or savings & loan institution will go along with. It well may be, however, that you are not about to become indebted to the extent that the lenders are willing to let you. This is a personal decision. You may be living a lifestyle that involves sports cars, the theater, fancy restaurants, and expensive vacations, and you are not willing to give up any of it. If there is not enough income to do it all, then you have some hard choices to make.

Before you chuck the idea of home ownership for all the other goodies in life, remember that your home is so much more than a consumable purchase! It is really a capital investment that you can use and enjoy while it appreciates and makes money for you.

A gourmet dinner can bring enjoyment for a few hours. A tropical vacation can be heaven for a few weeks. Neither will provide any tangible return on investment. On the other hand, you can enjoy home ownership day in and day out year after year and, at the same time, realize a fantastic return on your investment, and that is the third criteria to be satisfied in purchasing a home.

2
Unveiling the Mysteries of Financing

Prior to the late 1970's, comparing home mortgages was relatively easy. Almost all mortgages were fixed rate, so all you really needed to know was the interest rate, the term, how many points (if any) were being charged, and whether or not there was a prepayment penalty.

Since that time, the banking industry has experienced a serious economic crisis caused, at least partially, by the deregulation of that industry. As commercial banks and savings & loan associations had to suddenly compete with money market accounts at a time of double digit inflation, the repayment of fixed rate loans with interest rates less than those offered on some types of savings accounts caused many of these financial institutions to experience serious, and sometimes fatal, financial consequences.

As a result of all of this, new and innovative forms of long-term mortgage financing were sought and found. The major form of mortgage financing that has come out of all of this is called the adjustable rate mortgage (ARM). Along with the ARMs came a multitude of complex terms and conditions, many of which are not at all obvious to the unsophisticated prospective mortgagor. Furthermore, these complexities have led to what I con-

sider downright unscrupulous and deceitful advertising on the part of many lenders and particularly, many mortgage brokers.

ARM: ADJUSTABLE RATE MORTGAGE

Here is a comprehensive and in-depth analysis of the ten aspects of an adjustable rate mortgage (ARM), as well as a comparison between ARMs and fixed rate mortgages.

Ten Aspects of an ARM to Consider:

1. Initial interest rate
2. Grace period before first interest rate adjustment
3. Index as basis for interest rate adjustment
4. Interest spread (or Margin)
5. Annual or periodic interest rate cap
6. Total life-of-loan interest rate cap
7. Negative amortization
8. Silent journal
9. Loan assumption
10. Prepayment penalty

Initial Interest Rate

Unscrupulous advertising often comes into play here. Many lenders and/or mortgage brokers will make a big deal about low starting rates without discussing the other, equally important, aspects of the loan. This is not to say that a low starting rate is not important, because it is. However, it should be considered with all of the other aspects of the loan. For example, an ARM with an initial rate of 7.5% with the potential of escalating to 14% might not be as attractive as one with an 8% initial rate that caps out at 13%. When shopping for a loan, look for a good initial rate, but remember that there are other aspects to consider as well.

It should be pointed out here that most lending institutions qualify the borrower based upon the initial rate which, if you stop to think about it, does not make a great deal of sense. If you barely qualify for a loan at 8%, and then shortly thereafter we experience a sustained period of tight money and inflation and the rate goes up to 12% or more, you may find it extremely difficult, if not impossible, to meet the financial obligations of that mortgage. However, if you are young and can foresee significant upward mobility in your future earnings, then a low initial rate ARM may be your best and only way to get started in home ownership.

Grace Period

There is generally an initial period, which I like to refer to as the honeymoon period, before the lender can make the first interest rate adjustment on your loan. This period is typically either six months or one year. The longer the honeymoon period the better, because once it is over, most ARMs are going to adjust upward.

At the present time, there is an abundant supply of money and a number of lenders are offering an ARM with an initial fixed rate for as long as three to five years. Some of these are very attractive. The initial rates of these are usually somewhere be-

tween that of fixed rate mortgages and standard ARMs.

Index Bases

Once the honeymoon period is over, the interest that you will pay, subject to limitations to be discussed shortly, will be based on some fixed percentage above a particular index. The five indexes currently in use are: 1) six-month treasury bill rates, 2) one-year treasury, constant maturity, 3) three-year treasury, constant maturity, 4) five-year treasury, constant maturity, and 5) Federal Home Loan Bank (FHLB) district cost of funds.

Most savings & loan associations prefer to use the FHLB district cost of funds, since this is the federal banking system of which they are an integral part. Commercial banks and other lenders, including some S & L's, will offer one of the treasury indexes. A few will offer a choice of more than one index.

The difference from one to another of the indexes is a matter of stability and where the indexes stand at the time of the loan. The Federal Home Loan Bank has divided the United States into twelve districts, therefore the local district index will be affected partially by national influences and partially by local influences. Generally, this index is considered to be more stable in the short term than the various treasury indexes.

Recently, however, the one-year treasury index has stood at slightly over 6%, while the 11th district (California, Nevada, and Arizona) stood at slightly over 7%. With similar spreads (to be discussed momentarily), an interest rate based upon the one-year treasury index could prove to be significantly less expensive than one based upon the 11th district index. However, bankers are not stupid, so the loans based upon the treasury index usually have a greater spread to compensate for the lower index rate.

In order to fully analyze a given loan, it is imperative to know the index which will be used and its

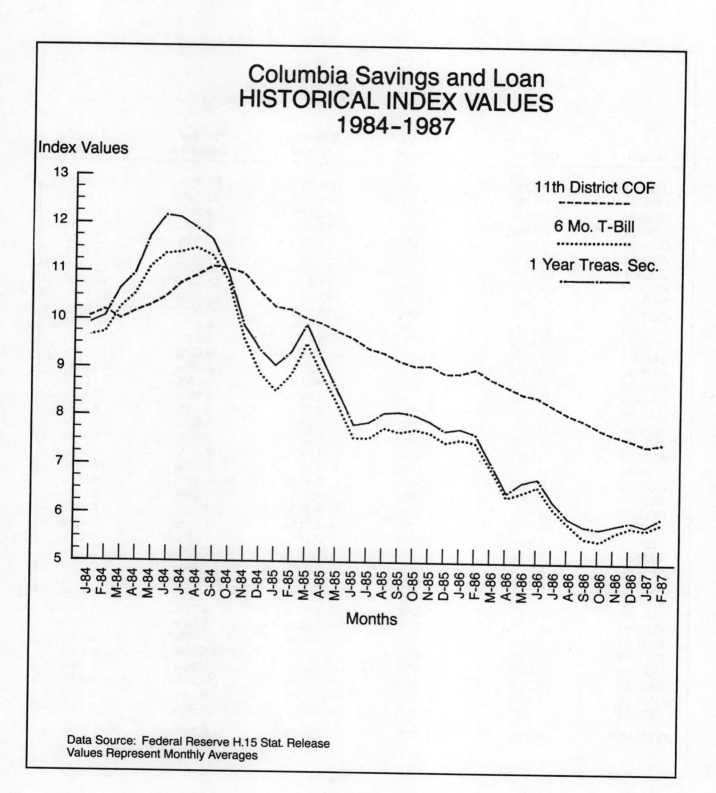

HISTORICAL INDEX VALUES

Month	11th District	6-Month Discount	6-Month Yield	1-Year Treasury	3-Year Treasury
JAN-84	10.03%	9.06%	9.63%	9.90%	10.93%
FEB-84	10.17%	9.13%	9.70%	10.04%	11.05%
MAR-84	9.98%	9.58%	10.21%	10.59%	11.59%
APR-84	10.14%	9.83%	10.49%	10.90%	11.98%
MAY-84	10.26%	10.31%	11.03%	11.66%	12.75%
JUN-84	10.43%	10.55%	11.30%	12.08%	13.18%
JUL-84	10.71%	10.58%	11.33%	12.03%	13.08%
AUG-84	10.86%	10.65%	11.41%	11.82%	12.50%
SEP-84	11.04%	10.51%	11.25%	11.58%	12.34%
OCT-84	10.99%	10.05%	10.74%	10.90%	11.85%
NOV-84	10.89%	8.99%	9.55%	9.82%	10.90%
DEC-84	10.52%	8.36%	8.85%	9.33%	10.56%
JAN-85	10.22%	8.03%	8.49%	9.02%	10.43%
FEB-85	10.16%	8.34%	8.83%	9.29%	10.55%
MAR-85	9.98%	8.92%	9.47%	9.86%	11.05%
APR-85	9.87%	8.31%	8.80%	9.14%	10.49%
MAY-85	9.70%	7.75%	8.18%	8.46%	9.75%
JUN-85	9.56%	7.16%	7.53%	7.80%	9.05%
JUL-85	9.36%	7.16%	7.53%	7.86%	9.18%
AUG-85	9.27%	7.35%	7.74%	8.05%	9.31%
SEP-85	9.12%	7.27%	7.65%	8.07%	9.37%
OCT-85	9.02%	7.32%	7.71%	8.01%	9.25%
NOV-85	9.03%	7.26%	7.64%	7.88%	8.88%
DEC-85	8.86%	7.08%	7.45%	7.68%	8.40%
JAN-86	8.77%	7.13%	7.51%	7.73%	8.41%
FEB-86	8.96%	7.08%	7.44%	7.61%	8.10%
MAR-86	8.74%	6.60%	6.92%	7.03%	7.30%
APR-86	8.59%	6.07%	6.35%	6.44%	6.86%
MAY-86	8.44%	6.16%	6.45%	6.65%	7.27%
JUN-86	8.37%	6.28%	6.57%	6.73%	7.41%
JUL-86	8.19%	5.85%	6.12%	6.27%	6.86%
AUG-86	8.02%	5.58%	5.82%	5.93%	6.49%
SEP-86	7.90%	5.31%	5.54%	5.77%	6.62%
OCT-86	7.72%	5.26%	5.48%	5.72%	6.56%
NOV-86	7.60%	5.42%	5.65%	5.80%	6.46%
DEC-86	7.51%	5.53%	5.76%	5.87%	6.43%
JAN-87	7.40%	5.47%	5.71%	5.78%	6.41%
FEB-87	7.45%	5.60%	5.84%	5.96%	6.56%
AVERAGE	**9.31%**	**7.70%**	**8.14%**	**8.44%**	**9.37%**

rate at the time the loan commitment is being made. The chart shown here compares the 11th District cost of funds, the six-month Treasury Bill, and the prime rate from January 1980 through October 1986.

Interest Spread or Margin

The spread is simply the difference between the amount of interest charged and the index rate. For example, if the 11th district index is 7.22% and the spread is 2.5%, then the interest charged will be 9.72%. Since normally the spread remains constant throughout the life of the loan, then as the index goes up, so goes the charged rate of interest. Similarly, as the index decreases, then the charged rate of interest will also go down.

Some lenders do not quote a spread per se. Instead, they make a loan commitment for a very short duration, usually not more than a week or ten days, and when the loan closes at whatever rate is in effect at the time, the spread is actually established as the difference between the original loan rate and the governing index rate at the time the loan closed. In essence, they back into the spread. This is preferable for one very important reason. In most ARMs, an initial interest rate is established along with an index and a spread. Invariably, the interest goes up, sometimes significantly, at the end of the honeymoon period, regardless of whether or not there have been any changes in the index during that period. For example, let's say that the 11th district index is 8.55%, the initial rate is 8%, the spread is 2%, the honeymoon period is one year, the loan amount is $100,000, and the term is thirty years. During the first year of this loan, the monthly payments will be $733.76. After the first year, assuming absolutely no change in the economy or the index, the new interest rate will be 10.55% (8.55% + 2%) and the new payments will be $918.48. This is a difference of $184.72, or a 25% increase in the monthly payment.

In the case where the spread was backed into at the time of closing, the interest rate in a mortgage that I placed was 8.75% instead of 8% for the exact situation just mentioned. The result, again assuming no change in the index, was a steady payment of $786.70 indefinitely. This amounts to $52.94 per month more than the initial payment on the first loan of $733.76. Since either loan is going to be affected similarly by changes in the index, then this seems to be a far more preferable loan from the borrower's point of view. Of course, if you were only planning to stay in the property for one or two years, then the first loan would be your best bet.

Annual or Periodic Interest Rate Cap

This is one of two caps to be concerned with. The periodic cap restricts the amount the interest can change per period, regardless of what the index does. A period is usually either six months or one year. If the period is one year, then the annual cap would typically be between 1% and 2%. If the period is six months, then the semi-annual cap would typically be between 0.5% and 1%. Assume an annual cap of 1.5%. If the index increases or decreases by 1.5% or more during the period, then the interest rate of the loan can increase or decrease, respectively, by a maximum of 1.5%. Assuming no negative amortization (to be discussed shortly), then the amortization schedule would be revised to reflect the new interest rate and hence, the new required payment.

Several things should be pointed out. If the index changes (either up or down) by less than the periodic cap, then the corresponding interest rate will change accordingly. Finally, it should be realized that the indexes actually do move in both directions. Most of us have become so used to prices, once raised, never coming down. Recently, we have seen that that is not the case with gasoline. Also, ARM loans placed several years ago are operating at lower rates and correspondingly lower payments today.

Total Life-of-Loan Interest Rate Cap

This cap defines the maximum amount a loan can increase or decrease over the life of the loan. Usually the figure is 5%, although sometimes it is less. The lifetime cap is usually figured from the initial rate, which is another reason why that starting rate can be very important. For example, a loan with a starting rate of 8% and a 5% cap theoretically could reach a maximum of 13% and fall to a minimum of 3%. If the loan was established at a period of an abundance of money and relatively low interest rates, then the chances of the rate dropping dramatically are slim to none. On the other hand, had the loan been established when money was tight and rates were high, say 14%, then it would be quite conceivable that it could eventually decrease by the full amount of the cap. Everyone in the business considers the lifetime cap as vital, since we can all feel inflation lurking in the shadows waiting to pounce and ravage once again.

Negative Amortization

Before we discuss negative amortization, I want to be sure that everyone understands the concept of an amortized repayment schedule.

Let's use an example. A loan for $1,200.00 for one year at 12% interest is payable at $100.00 plus interest on the unpaid balance. At the end of the first month, the payment will be $112.00 ($100.00 + 1% of $1,200.00). Next month, the payment will be $111.00 ($100.00 + 1% of $1,100.00). The following month, the payment will be $110.00, and so on.

A fully amortized repayment schedule utilizes a very complicated mathematical formula that allows the monthly payments to remain constant throughout the life of the loan, with each payment applying a portion to principal and a portion to interest. In the early stages, most of the payment is applied to interest with very little reducing the principal, but with each payment a little more is applied to principal and a little less is applied to interest, until finally the very last payment contains almost no interest and fully pays the remaining balance owing against the principal.

The discussion thus far has not considered the theory of negative amortization. Negative amortization occurs when there exists, in addition to the other caps, a cap on the amount payments can be increased from period to period. The usual figure is 7.5%. Let's develop an example to help understand what happens to cause negative amortization.

Let's reconsider the $100,000 loan at 8%, only this time let's consider a 1.5% annual cap and a 7.5% payment increase cap. As we noted earlier, the payments during the initial period on this loan would be $733.76 per month. Assuming an index change of the full 1.5% for the next period, the mortgage payment should increase to $840.85 per month to cover principal and interest. However, since there is a 7.5% payment cap, the payments can only be increased to $788.79 per month. This represents a short fall of $52.06 per month, which is added to the principal balance. This is called negative amortization, which simply means that the amount that you owe on your loan actually grows instead of diminishing each month, even though you faithfully make your payments month in and month out.

This presents, in my opinion, a very undesirable situation. Banks go for this because they figure that homes will appreciate faster than the negative amortization will build up. Although the payments are limited to 7.5% increases, which has been chosen because it tends to correspond to expected annual raises, several things can happen to mess up the theory. First, the buyer is usually into this kind of loan with a minimum down. So if the bank is wrong and the property does not appreciate as fast as the negative amortization builds up, pretty soon the buyer may owe more than the property is worth. Furthermore, annual raises are not so automatic anymore. As buyers face economic hard times and decreasing or nonexistent equity, they will have very little incentive to carry out their end of the bargain. In Houston, hundreds of such homes have simply been abandoned, leaving behind nothing but the keys and a note saying, "Sorry. Just can't hack it anymore."

There may be a particular circumstance where a negative amortization loan might be the right way to go, but generally speaking, I think it should be avoided like the plague. Fewer and fewer of these loans are being offered as banks have now experienced some of the negative effects.

Silent Journal

Most people, including a lot who profess to be real estate professionals, have never heard of this one. I have heard it described by other terms, but what is important is to make sure that your loan does not have it. This is how silent journal works: suppose your ARM loan is based upon a fairly volatile index. Further suppose that the index goes up for the period 2.5% but you have a periodic cap of 2.0%.

Now suppose the index continues to rise another 1.5% the next period. With silent journal, any excess between the cap and the actual index increase (or decrease) can be carried over to the next period. With or without silent journal, an 8% loan would increase 2.0% to 10.0% even though the index rose 2.5%.

During the next period, it would rise to 11.5% if there was no silent journal. However, if the loan had silent journal, the interest rate during this second adjustment period would be to 12.0%, since they would add on the 0.5% carry-over that could not be charged the previous period because of the 2.0% periodic cap. If this sounds confusing, it is. The important thing is, most reputable lenders are

no longer using silent journal, so it should not be difficult to find a loan without it. Just remember to ask. Most lenders will be very impressed that you have even heard of it.

Loan Assumption

Most ARMs are assumable, but it is important to be sure that your particular loan is also. This could be extremely important if, when you are ready to sell, the economy is experiencing a period of tight money and high interest rates. Your assumable mortgage could then be very competitive and desirable and a definite asset in getting top dollar for your home.

Assumable or not, you still have to come up with a buyer who qualifies, and even though the buyer takes over the first responsibility for the repayment of this loan, you are very often still secondarily responsible in case the buyer defaults. This is a very good reason to make sure that the buyer puts down a sufficient amount of cash. This way, he will have a significant vested interest in the property so as to be motivated not to default. And in the rare instance when the buyer defaults in spite of the fact that he is well vested, there will be significant equity for you to take over the property and resell it in order to protect your interest. Incidentally, most fixed rate loans now being written are not assumable.

Prepayment Penalty

Many loans will incorporate a penalty for paying off the loan before the mortgage period is up, especially if they are written during a time of high interest rates. There are a variety of formulas for deriving the prepayment penalty. Most penalties are a percentage, usually between 1% and 2%, of the principal balance of the loan at the time of prepayment.

Some loans waive the prepayment penalty after the loan has been in force a certain period of time, often five years. Other loans keep the penalty in effect throughout the life of the loan, but incorporate a formula that decreases the impact of the penalty as time goes on. Some lending institutions will waive the prepayment penalty if the new loan on the property is placed with them.

Currently, most ARM loans and some fixed rate loans are being written without prepayment penalties. This is because interest rates are low and most lenders do not anticipate that they will go much lower, so that there is nothing all that attractive for them to protect at the moment. As interest rates rise, prepayment penalties become more prevalent. It is certainly wise to avoid prepayment penalties whenever possible.

ARM SUMMARY

As can easily be seen, an adjustable rate mortgage is complex. Determining the right loan for you depends upon several factors.

First, if you are just going to squeak through from the standpoint of qualifying, then the choices may be reduced to the loans with the lowest rates. If you only plan to be in the house involved for a relatively short period of time, then you want the loan that will be the least expensive during the early years. If you plan to plant roots for the long haul, then the long-term effects of the loan should be of greater concern.

Finally, your perception of the economic future will have a great deal to do with not only what type of ARM, but whether to go for a fixed rate mortgage or an ARM. If you feel that the rates are about as low as they are going to get, then you will probably want to lock in a fixed rate. If you feel that the economy is going to remain stable or that the rates will even go lower, then you may prefer the lower initial costs of an ARM. Everyone's situation is unique and should be treated as such.

OTHER TYPES OF LOANS

Fixed Rate Loans

Compared to an ARM, little needs to be said about a fixed rate loan. Most are amortized for the life of the loan, usually fifteen or thirty years. Some are written with a balloon payment after a certain time period, such as ten years. More about this can be found in the section on Creative Financing.

The major distinction of a fixed rate mortgage is, as the name implies, that the rate established at the time the loan was originated remains fixed for the life of the loan.

Several disadvantages that often accompany a fixed rate mortgage are the fact that they are usually not assumable and that they often have a prepayment penalty. However, a good fixed rate loan is certainly preferable to an ARM. The only problem is that they are becoming considerably more difficult to obtain.

Open End Loan

An open end loan means simply that additional funds can be borrowed on that loan sometime in the future based upon a formula devised at the time the loan was originated. For example, let's say that you originally borrow $80,000 based upon an appraisal and sale price of $100,000. This is an 80% loan.

Now let's say that the open end provision states that you may borrow up to 80% of the appraised value any time in the future under the same terms and conditions that the loan was originally written. In ten years, you may have a child ready for college and need cash to pay for his or her education. It might be reasonable to assume that by this time the home is worth $150,000, and the loan principal has been reduced to approximately $73,000. You can now borrow 80% of the new appraised value, or $120,000. If you subtract the

$73,000 principal balance, this would give you $47,000 in cash for your child's education. If an open end option is available, it should be considered in light of its future potential value.

Easy Qualifier Loan

Generally speaking, with a down payment of 25% or more, many lending institutions offer what they call an easy qualifier loan. With such a large down payment, the bank feels that its collateral position is secure because of the large equity the borrower has in the property from the very beginning.

Therefore, the bank is willing to make the loan based only on an appraisal and a satisfactory credit report. There is no requirement for employment and bank account verifications, proof of prior years' earnings, etc. Such a loan can be approved very quickly, often in less than a week.

Although speed is sometimes a factor, such a loan is often sought because the borrower would have difficulty qualifying for a conventional 80% loan. This might be the case if the borrower was self-employed and had not been in business long enough to establish an earnings record satisfactory to the loan underwriter. It must be remembered, however, that the borrower must have a good credit background in order to qualify for this or any other loan.

One would think that the interest rate would be more favorable if the borrower puts more down against an easy qualifier loan. This is generally not true. When the lending institution is being a little more lax in credit requirements, they will normally charge about ¼% more for an easy qualifier.

Secondary Mortgage Market

Without turning this into a course in financing, it is important to understand where mortgage funding comes from. There are several places the borrower can go to seek a mortgage: commercial banks, savings & loan associations, mortgage brokers, mortgage bankers, and individuals (more about this under Creative Financing). The great majority of mortgages originated by these sources (with the possible exception of individuals) are sold to what is referred to as the secondary mortgage market.

The Federal National Mortgage Association (FNMA), referred to affectionately as "Fanny Mae," represents the backbone of the secondary mortgage market. The FNMA is a privately funded corporation chartered and backed by the federal government for the purpose of buying FHA, VA, and conventional conforming loans from loan originators. The FNMA has strict and uniform requirements regarding credit, the appraisal, and the loan "package" in general which must be met in order to sell a loan to them. Fanny Mae is a profitable and self-supporting operation.

There are many other players in the secondary mortgage market. They include insurance companies, retirement funds, mutual funds, and real estate investment trusts. These entities are major factors in purchasing loans that do not conform to Fanny Mae requirements. They all tend to require the same format in packaging the loan as has been established by Fanny Mae.

You might be wondering at this point just how the loan originator makes his money if he sells the loan just as soon as it closes. The answer is points and discount fees. This is why mortgage brokers can compete with commercial banks and savings & loan associations. They are all doing the same thing, acting as mortgage brokers. There are some differences, however. First, many S & L's keep their adjustable rate mortgages in their own portfolios. Mortgage brokers often represent lending institutions that are also going to sell the loan, therefore they have to include an additional fee in order to get paid for their efforts. Unfortunately, a mixed bag of individuals has been drawn to the mortgage brokerage business, and the result has generally left a bad taste in the mouths of most knowledgeable real estate agents. Even under the very best of circumstances, the mortgage broker is the inevitable middleman, and is continually in the position of burning the candle at both ends.

His clients, the lenders, are constantly changing terms and conditions and very often will not back the broker on commitments that he has already made to a prospective purchaser. For these reasons, I try to avoid mortgage brokers, but occasionally they are able to come up with a loan that cannot be found by shopping around with the local lenders.

Conforming Loan

A conforming loan is one that meets all of the Fanny Mae criteria. As of this writing, this also includes a maximum loan limit of $187,600. A conforming loan will usually enjoy a preferential interest rate since the loan originator is guaranteed a secondary market purchase of that loan.

FHA & VA Loans

FHA loans are government insured and available to anyone. VA loans are government guaranteed and available to qualified veterans. The maximum amount of an FHA loan varies from one locale to another. In Contra Costa County, California, the maximum was $90,000 as of July, 1987. The maximum VA guarantee was $130,000 ($110,000 if it represents 100% financing). At that moment, each loan had a base interest rate of 9.5% and a 6.75 point discount. This means that when you borrow $100,000, you will only receive $93,250 ($100,000 less discount of $6,750).

In addition, there are loan origination fees. For the VA loan, the loan origination fee is 2%. For the FHA loan, the fee is 1%. The discount on the VA loan is fixed and must be paid by the seller. The discount on the FHA loan is flexible and can be paid by either buyer or seller or shared by both.

If the interest rate is raised, say to 10% at this point in time, then the discount would be reduced to about 3.5%. These figures change constantly with market conditions.

There are three major disadvantages to these types of loans. First of all, in many parts of the country, the limits are too low relative to the price of housing. Next, the regulated interest rate is lower than market, therefore the lenders have to charge an exorbitant discount fee to make up the difference. Finally, many lending institutions simply will not put up with the extra paper work and red tape required to deal with these agencies. In addition, the VA loan is only available to qualified veterans.

The main advantage of these loans is that they provide 90% to 100% financing. The second advantage is that they are assumable.

Jumbo Loans

A jumbo loan is any loan larger than the maximum Fanny Mae limit, which is currently $187,600. These loans usually command a slightly higher interest rate than a conforming loan since they do not have a guaranteed secondary market. However, the vast majority of these loans, if properly packaged, have little difficulty finding their way into the secondary market.

PRIVATE MORTGAGE INSURANCE

Many lending institutions will not make conventional loans greater than 80% without requiring private mortgage insurance (PMI). PMI insures the amount of the loan in excess of 80% up to a maximum of 95%. There are various plans available, but on average, it costs the borrower about ½% of the principal balance and is payable until that principal balance is reduced to 80%. Unfortunately, PMI does not take into consideration that a property may appreciate and within a relatively short time the loan may not represent more than 80% of its appreciated value. In this case, the only way to get rid of the PMI premiums would be to refinance, which may or may not be economically prudent at the time. PMI is an added expense that should be avoided if possible.

CREATIVE FINANCING

Everyone has heard the term "creative financing," but very few know what it really means. In home buying, it usually means working out a way for the seller to participate in the financing so that you both benefit.

In order for a seller to be able to consider financing, he must be in such a position that he does not need the proceeds of the sale for another specific purpose. If you can find a seller in that position, a major incentive for his taking back the financing might be the reduced capital gain taxes he would pay as a result of the sale.

The IRS charges a capital gains tax on the sale of all real estate. This tax is computed as the difference between the sale price less sales expense and the purchase price plus the cost of improvements. At present, this is taxed at the same rate as the taxpayer's income tax. This can be a very significant tax.

However, if the seller takes back financing, he will only pay capital gain taxes each year on the amount received during that year. Under the proper circumstances, by spreading this tax liability over a number of years, the actual amount of taxes paid can be greatly reduced; and the seller, rather than the government, has the use of the money for a longer period of time.

It should be noted that this tax can be deferred indefinitely on one's primary residence provided you buy another primary residence for a equal or greater cost within two years of the sale. This is discussed in greater detail at the end of the next section.

The buyer may be able to obtain a preferential rate of interest from the seller as an inducement to buy his property, and sellers usually do not ask for points. There are some IRS limitations as to how far the seller can go below the competitive interest rate market without being penalized.

In times of high interest rates, a seller might be forced to take back the financing in order to effect a sale. In such cases it is common to request a balloon payment somewhere down the line.

For example, a seller might take back a mortgage but may not want to wait thirty years to get fully paid, especially if he is getting on in years. In this case, he may agree to take the mortgage amortized for thirty years in order to keep the payments down, but insist upon a balloon payment of the entire principal due at the end of ten years. This might be quite acceptable to the buyers if they feel that at the end of ten years the home will have appreciated greatly and they will have no problem obtaining new financing through conventional sources at that time.

Another way of involving the seller in creative financing is to have him take back a secondary mortgage behind a conventional bank loan. There are limits to what the lending institution in the first position will allow. The norm is 80/10/10. This means that the primary lending institution makes a conventional 80% loan. The seller takes back a second mortgage for 10% and the buyer makes a down payment of 10%. There could be several advantages to such an arrangement: no PMI, no points on the part the seller takes, easier qualifying for the first loan, and possibly a better interest rate on the second if the seller is really anxious.

I recently did a variation of this for a young doctor with great financial upward mobility but limited cash at the time. We obtained a 75% easy qualifier loan from a lending institution because the doctor had not been in practice long enough to have an established earning record. We also secured a 15% second mortgage from the seller (with the approval of the primary lender), interest only for seven years with the principal all due and payable at that time. This got the doctor into a home he could not otherwise afford for only 10% down, payments he could handle in the early stages, and a balloon payment that he was confident he could meet without difficulty when the time came.

Most sellers rightfully become very leery of getting involved in financing when the buyer ends up with less than 10% of his own cash involved. In such cases, it might be possible to work out a lease with an option to purchase or a contract to purchase.

Lease/Option

In the case of the lease/option, an agreement is drawn whereupon the prospective buyer leases the property for a specified period of time, say one year. In addition, the prospective buyer is given the option to purchase the property for a specific amount at some future point in time. Usually, that would be either any time during the lease period or at the end of the lease period.

The advantage of a lease/option is that you can lock up the price to make a purchase at some future time. This privilege, however, is usually not free. Some amount of option money, to be negotiated, would normally be required to "buy" the option privilege. This amount could be anywhere from very little to as much as 10%. If you decide to exercise your option, then the option money is applied toward the purchase price. If you do not or can not exercise the option, then the option money is lost. Therefore, you should not consider entering into a lease/option unless you know you'll be able to exercise that option when the day of reckoning arrives.

There are several ways a lease/option can be set up. If the lease portion is just a straight lease, there is no purchasing power or tax advantages to the arrangement. You would simply be renting until some future point in time when you feel that you

are in a better financial position to buy for a purchase price already locked in place.

A more attractive way to set up the lease/option would be to apply at least some portion of the lease payments toward the purchase price. In this way, you would be building equity toward the down payment. This is obviously advantageous to the prospective buyer, but it might also be attractive to the seller. If the lease payments are considered rent, then they are taxed as ordinary income to the seller. On the other hand, any portion that is applied to the purchase price would ultimately be part of a capital gain (or loss), and might provide preferential tax treatment. This advantage, however, has diminished considerably with the tax law placed into effect in 1987.

Lease/options are almost always set up because the prospective buyer cannot come up with a sufficient cash down payment at the time that he wants to take possession of the property. Possibly a somewhat better solution to this dilemma would be a "contract of sale."

Contract of Sale

With a contract of sale, you enter into a legally binding contract to purchase the property with all of the terms of how the payments are going to be made clearly spelled out. The major difference from a normal purchase is that title does not change hands. The seller continues to own the property until some point in the future when all of the terms of the contract of sale are met. This is only fair since the buyer would be making less than an acceptable down payment in order to take possession of the property.

A contract of sale can be recorded just as a deed or mortgage can, and it is wise to do so. This puts future lien holders on notice that such a contract is in existence, but the major disadvantage for the buyer is that an unscrupulous or financially pressed seller could, either voluntarily or involuntarily, let liens pile up against the property to the point that the property may be lost to foreclosure or that he could not otherwise hold up his end of the contract and deliver a free and clear title to the buyer at the appropriate time. It is important, therefore, that the buyer know the reputation and integrity of the seller before entering into a contract of sale.

Aside from the disadvantage mentioned above, this can be a very nice way to purchase a property when you do not have enough cash to come up with a sufficient down payment. A number of years ago, I purchased a property in Connecticut under a contract of sale which spelled out terms over a five year period. At the end of the period, I would take title provided all of the terms had been met. As it turned out, I was offered an opportunity in California that I could not refuse, so I put the property up for sale. You might ask, how can you sell something you don't own? You can, as long as in the process you meet all of the terms of the contract of sale.

In my particular case, the purchase price under the contract of sale was $125,000. At the end of three years, when I sold the property, I owed slightly less than $120,000. The property sold for $178,000. Title transferred directly from the original owner to my buyer, the owner was paid what was owed to her out of the proceeds, and I walked away with over $58,000. In the interim, my family and I enjoyed a wonderful place to live for only a little more than it would have cost to rent something comparable.

YOUR LEGAL RIGHTS AND RESPONSIBILITIES

You should always consult an attorney when legal advice is required. The laws vary from state to state and it would be impossible to provide accurate advice here.

It is also appropriate to point out that in the sec-

tions to follow, numerous legal documents will be utilized as examples.

The documents that you will be confronted with will probably look different in both form and content. You may find, after these discussions, that the forms being utilized in your area seem grossly inadequate. If this is the case and you are truly concerned, you can either ask that certain paragraphs be added, or you can hire an attorney to prepare the forms for you. You do not have to sign forms that you are not comfortable with.

Whether these documents are prepared by an attorney or a real estate agent, they are legally binding documents that are an integral part of buying a home. The way these documents are structured is extremely important both in protecting your legal rights and limiting your liabilities. Many legal complications can arise in the course of buying a home. The legal documents used in completing these transactions are constantly being refined and improved to reflect the changing needs of our increasingly complex society. The local boards of realtors, with great assistance from both the state and national associations of realtors, labor endlessly in an effort to produce forms that will eliminate ambiguity and clearly define each party's rights and responsibilities in the transaction.

The forms, however, are only a good guideline for avoiding future problems. They are really of very little value if they are sloppily or incompletely prepared. This is where a really professional agent earns that commission. As we shall see shortly, the way these forms are prepared can either properly define the terms of the transaction and protect the rights of the parties concerned, or result in devastation for one or more of the parties concerned.

The real purpose of all of these documents is to spell out the true intent of all of the parties in the transaction. If the true intent of any of the parties is devious or in any way different than that proclaimed, then problems are likely to arise no matter how great a set of documents you have.

The keys to a successful transaction? Intent and motivation. If you have a motivated seller who fully intends to sell a home and a motivated buyer who fully intends to fulfill that end of the bargain, then somehow the transaction will close and everyone will part at least reasonably satisfied. However, if one of the parties is playing games and not being straight, then the whole transaction is flirting with disaster. Again, the various documents are designed to help avoid the problems that can arise from such a situation, but an experienced and knowledgeable agent can usually sense and find ways to combat these situations before they get out of hand.

Again, let me emphasize: if you do not feel completely comfortable with what you are being asked to sign, see an attorney first.

3
The Search Is On

WORKING WITH YOUR AGENT

Another area of confusion for many buyers concerns legal and/or moral obligations to their agents. Let me set the tone of this discussion right away by saying that a great many people display absolutely no remorse whatsoever in utilizing an agent's knowledge, time, gasoline, etc., and then discarding the person with no thought of the commission that won't be earned. As a result, it is little wonder that agents do everything possible to protect themselves from such occurrences.

It is when the agent goes beyond the normal safeguards of preservation that the buyer should beware. Many agents feel very possessive about any prospective buyer, regardless of the circumstances under which they have met. If you walk into or call a real estate office seeking information, you will normally be directed to the "floor agent." This is the agent on duty at that particular time, gladly fulfilling his or her duty in the hopes of meeting a prospective buyer or seller. If this agent seems knowledgeable and you feel reasonably comfortable, then there is no reason not to work with him. The important thing to remember, however, is that you have no obligation at this point in time to this agent.

Now let's say that this agent takes you out and shows you several houses and you decide to buy one. You still have no legal obligation to this agent. However, your moral obligation is growing.

Generally speaking, the agent looks to the seller to pay the commission. However, there are plenty of buyers out there who will use an agent to find the right property and then attempt to go directly to the seller, cutting the agent out of the transaction in the hopes of making a better deal on a direct basis.

Depending on the type of listing (more about this in the section on selling), this may or may not be legally possible. The point being, agents are put in a position of having to do everything possible to protect their legal claim to be compensated for work performed.

This gets us into the area of procuring cause. In the past, and this may be true in some areas today, the agent who first showed the property was considered the procuring cause and would generally prevail at a board of realtors arbitration. Today, at least in most areas, the agent who produces the signed offer to purchase is generally considered the procuring cause.

Because the payment of commissions is generally the responsibility of the seller, this subject will be developed more fully in the section devoted to sellers. The subject has been brought up here to point out that there is usually no good economic reason to cut the real estate agent out of the transaction, and there are plenty of valid reasons to keep him in there looking out for your best interests.

Now let's go back to the same scenario. The agent has shown you a number of houses, one of which you think you might like to buy. However, as you get to know this agent, you realize that you just do not feel comfortable with him or her. This is a difficult situation. It is hard to tell someone that you don't like working with them. So what do you do? You can simply walk away and find another agent to work with. Sometimes buyers find themselves in such an uncomfortable situation that they just can't wait to get away, no matter what.

A better solution, however, might be to broach the subject. You will get one of several responses, possibly anger or defensiveness. If the agent reacts in any way whatsoever that adds to your discomfort, then tell him firmly that you do not need the aggravation and you wish to terminate the relationship immediately.

If, however, the agent apologizes and suggests that you might be more comfortable with another individual, you might have a solution to the problem. Usually, the manager will be brought in, and a new agent will be selected with great care to work with you from that point on. Also, the agent you have left will normally be paid a referral fee out of any resulting commission, so everyone ends up reasonably happy.

Selecting an Agent

A dive into a dark and murky pond that is unfamiliar can be full of surprises and quite dangerous. The same is true of entering the real estate market.

I definitely suggest that you work through an agent and that you start out by selecting that agent with care. Many people select agents because they are friends or relatives. This is not necessarily the best choice unless you know that particular friend or relative is truly a professional in the real estate field. Would you allow someone to perform bypass surgery on you simply because he was a friend? Or would you have someone represent you in a multi-million dollar libel suit because she was a relative?

Maybe you would, but I sure wouldn't. In either case, I would search out the very best in the field before I made such an important decision. Since you are considering purchasing what very likely could become your largest asset, isn't the selection of your real estate agent just as important as choosing a surgeon or an attorney?

The best way to find a top-notch agent is through the recommendation of someone who has had a good experience with that agent. Even then, I would want to ask some probing questions before embarking on a real estate search with that person. These questions will be discussed momentarily.

Assuming that you are new to the area, or at least to the business of buying a home in the area, then you will have to take a few steps in order to hook up with a good professional agent.

The first thing that you probably will do is start looking at real estate ads in the newspaper and the *Homes* magazines that are given away at local grocery stores, motels, etc. You may make your first contacts with real estate agents as a result of calling about one or more of these ads. This, of course, results in chance meetings with agents.

A more systematic way to get in touch with agents is to check out the real estate community by talking to knowledgeable people around town. Talk to several banks. They will usually give you the names of several firms to contact. Almost anyone who has been in the community for some time will have an opinion as to which firms have the best reputations. However, these are still only opinions which may or may not be based on anything more than rumors or gut feelings, but at least that is more than you have to go on at the very beginning.

Next, when you do approach a real estate agency, you might first ask for the manager. Tell him what you are looking for in an agent. You might still end up with the floor agent, but very often when a prospective buyer walks in and shows that he is knowledgeable and knows what he wants, the manager will not risk hooking him up with an inexperienced agent, even if that agent does have the duty at that time and would otherwise expect that the prospective buyer be turned over to him.

Certain questions should be asked. How long has the agent been in the real estate business? Does he have specific knowledge of the area in which you are interested? How many transactions has he successfully closed? Would he be willing to give you the names of several satisfied clients as personal recommendations? These recommendations should be checked and you should be totally satisfied with the answers you have received. If that is the case, you now have an agent with whom you should be able to work and feel comfortable.

What Your Agent Needs to Know

In order for your agent to do a job for you, you will have to reveal a lot of things that you may consider very personal and private.

The first area has to do with finances, and most people are reluctant to divulge this information in great detail to a perfect stranger. Sooner or later, the agent is going to have to learn a great deal about your money to serve you properly, but the smart agent understands your reluctance and is willing to work on small amounts of information at a time while you are in the process of getting to know one another.

For starters, the agent must know the price range

that you can afford. You may not know this exactly yourself, therefore the agent will need to know a great deal more in order to arrive at a price you can afford. Your agent will need to know how much cash you have for a down payment and closing costs and will need to know your gross income and long term debts to determine the amount of mortgage for which you can qualify. Your future income potential may also be important if you are reaching to or slightly beyond your present limits for that home of your dreams. The sooner you give this information, the sooner the agent will be on the track and in sync with your needs. However, you will have to release this information as your own comfort level allows.

One of the worst possible things that can happen, from everyone's point of view, is to have the agent show a prospective buyer properties that are too expensive. Invariably the buyers will see something that they fall in love with, but sadly realize that they cannot afford. Usually, from this point on, they wistfully compare everything else with the dream home they cannot afford, and more often than not, the mission is doomed. Everyone would have been much better off if the buyers had been shown only properties they could afford. This is a compelling reason to get the economics out on the table at the earliest possible time.

The next area of information involves lifestyle. This is usually a lot more fun to talk about, but even here there are some things that are not easily discussed with strangers. For instance, if you have a passion to go skinny dipping in the pool, it might be helpful if the agent knew, but a little embarrassing to talk about. However, the agent will eventually get the message if you always check out the neighbors' windows relative to their view of the pool area.

The important things, of course, have to do with present or proposed family size. The number, age, and sex of children is important in determining the ideal number of bedrooms and baths required.

School districts are often an important consideration. Travel distances to work, schools, and shopping are factors. The neighborhood mix can also be a factor, although there is no guarantee that it will stay the same over time.

In order for the agent to be well-equipped to help you find your dream home, he is going to have to be privy to some of your innermost dreams and aspirations. By the time you are finished, your agent is going to know you very well, and could become a good friend for many years to come.

Finally, it is important that you understand the agent's fiduciary responsibility in a real estate transaction. In most areas of the country, the law states that the agent owes a fiduciary responsibility to whomever pays the commission, which invariably is the seller. This includes not only the listing agent, but also the selling agent who is considered a sub-agent of the listing agent; the commission, paid by the seller, is split in some manner between the two agents.

So where does this leave the buyer? Legally, in my opinion, in most parts of the country the buyer does not really have an agent who truly represents him. This leads to the age-old term *caveat emptor,* or "buyer beware." Practically speaking, most professional agents representing buyers will properly protect that buyer's best interest, even though legal fiduciary responsibility goes to the seller.

In California, the California Association of Realtors in general and various local boards in particular have made great strides in alleviating the compromising position in which the buyer's agent finds himself. The state law still maintains its definition of fiduciary responsibility, but additional laws have been passed to protect the buyer, requiring a great deal of disclosure, and somewhat allowing for separate agency, although there remains a conflict between the letter of the law and the practice condoned by the real estate commissioner. More will be said about this later when we get into the purchase contract.

LOOKING FOR YOUR DREAM HOUSE

Now that you have an agent to work with and you understand the financial realities of what you can afford, it is time to search out your dream home, or something as close as you can get to your dream given the restraints of your financial capabilities.

At this point, you may or may not have specific ideas about just what you are looking for. If your specifications are too exacting, you may find that they far exceed your budget. Therefore, in the beginning, it is better to keep as much of an open mind as possible until you have the opportunity to discover just what the market that you can afford has to offer.

Assuming a completely open mind, the logical first step is to get an overview of several neighborhoods to see what each has to offer. In this step, as in the steps to follow, it is important to pay close attention to the prices and what you get for the money. As you see the various properties, ask your agent questions about pricing, even if you are not especially interested in a particular property. This is your education in fair market value, and if you go about it properly, in a very short time you will be able to recognize a good value when you see it.

When you look at a property, ask the agent if the property is priced right, and if there are any comparables that have sold recently to substantiate that opinion. I guarantee that this will keep the agent on his toes and show that you are not another yokel from Podunk.

It may take several trips to the various neighborhoods before you are ready to settle on one in particular. Or you may find that any one of several neighborhoods would do providing you can find the right house.

Once the neighborhood(s) has been settled, it is time to start honing in on specifics. In order for your agent to get a sense of your needs, it is vitally important for you to vocalize the things you do and do not like about each house you see. Most of the better real estate agents are quite perceptive, but they are not mind readers. Don't be afraid to talk negatives as well as positives. Naturally, these discussions should not be held in front of the owners, but they will go a long way in helping the agent discover your tastes and desires. One caution: be sure that your criticisms are not the result of a champagne taste and a beer pocketbook. Be realistic in your expectations.

It would be very rare if some compromises did not have to be made in the course of purchasing a home. Either you are going to have to pay more than originally anticipated or you are going to have to settle for less. If the additional cost is still within your financial comfort level, then you probably should go for it. Otherwise, you may regret the decision to take something less and never be happy with what you end up with.

On the other hand, if you are already close to your financial limit, then don't even think about stretching it any further. Lower your sights somewhat, and if you cannot be totally happy with what you have to settle for, then think of it as a stepping stone to something a bit more grand sometime down the road. When you are really feeling that you are making a serious compromise, that is the time to be all the more sure that you are at least making a good financial investment.

The folks who make the best buys in homes are very often the ones who can see beyond that which is staring them in the face. These are relatively rare individuals who can picture a home, not as it is now decorated and furnished, but as they would decorate and furnish it to their own tastes.

I never cease to be amazed at how few people seem to have this ability. It has absolutely been proven that a home that is neat, clean, and attractively decorated will sell for significantly more than an identical home that is not as attractive in appearance.

If you can train yourself to ignore the ugly furni-

ture, the hideous wallpaper, or the grotesque chandelier, then you have taken a giant step in recognizing the potential that others may fail to see.

Houses Sell Houses

The basic popular suburban home consists of three bedrooms, two baths, kitchen, and living room with a dining area. A separate dining room is a real plus. The addition of a family room or family room/kitchen combination adds real value, as does a fourth bedroom or an additional half bath. One bath private to the master bedroom is very desirable. An eat-in kitchen or breakfast nook adds another attractive feature. A garage is also considered very important. In the better neighborhoods, it usually needs to be capable of housing two cars. In many climates, it is almost imperative. In the more temperate climates, a carport will often suffice.

Certain things within a home add more value than others. Kitchens top the list. Bathrooms come next and closet space is probably third. Amenities such as a fireplace, nice landscaping, a fenced yard, and built-in appliances are definitely desirable and add value. The value of swimming pools usually does not balance out with the cost. Things like intercoms, security systems, and automatic garage door operators are nice, but probably do not add a great deal of value to the selling price of the home.

Adding more than four bedrooms definitely has diminishing returns. A two-bedroom house might fit your needs very comfortably, but its resale value will be considerably less than an otherwise comparable three-bedroom house.

Sensible floor plans are very important. A house with little or no hallway area will undoubtedly necessitate passing through one room to get to another. This can be awkward. On the other hand, excessive hallway space adds to the square footage and thus the cost of a house in areas that cannot be well utilized.

House styles are also important. Traditional styles such as ranch homes, colonials, and Cape Cods are universally the most popular. In some areas, especially resort areas, rustic contemporary homes with large expanses of glass are very popular, but contemporary homes per se have never really caught on in a big way, and are often difficult to sell. Many contemporary designers felt compelled to be on the leading edge of technology, and the result was experimental housing.

For example, during the late 1950's and early 1960's, a lot of homes were given concrete slab floors with radiant heat pipes running through the slab. Hot water circulated through the pipes, warming the concrete which in turn radiated the heat throughout the house. Wall-to-wall carpeting or linoleum or tile was then laid over the slab. The biggest problem that these homes have presented over the years has been a failure in the radiant heating system. If the pipes embedded in the concrete break or get clogged, then the system usually has to be abandoned in favor of a new makeshift heating system for which the house was not really designed. A secondary problem is that the slab floors are very tiring on the legs.

Other contemporary designs have been utilized to conserve on building costs, with varying degrees of success. Still others have apparently been designed with no other purpose in mind than to be different.

This is not to say that there are not some really great contemporary homes around, because there are. However, most of the really great contemporaries are found in the upper end market rather than in the low to medium priced tract homes.

Finally, potentially adverse conditions could exist that are not readily apparent. The most universal of these are termites and dry rot. A pest control inspection should be an integral part of any house purchase. Such an inspection should cover dry rot caused by water leakage as well as bugs (termites, beetles, etc.).

Foundations can often have very serious problems which may be extremely expensive to correct. These problems could be the result of a faulty installation in the first place or unstable soil conditions. In either event, a thorough check of the foundation by a competent contractor or engineer should also be a part of a purchase agreement.

Roofs wear out. The age and condition should be ascertained. Plumbing, heating, and electrical systems also get tired after time and require expensive repairs or replacement. The same is true for kitchen appliances.

Even here in the San Francisco Bay area, one of the most expensive housing markets in the United States, one can obtain all of the necessary inspections, performed by competent individuals, for less than $500.00. This is a small price to pay for the peace of mind of knowing that you are not going to be faced with literally thousands of dollars worth of hidden expenses sometime down the road.

Now that we know what to look for and what to avoid, let's consider the basic four elements that make up value in residential real estate. They are location, price, terms, and condition. To say that one is more important than another would be foolish. However, they often have to be ordered according to your individual circumstances. For example, your budget and the size home you require may not allow you to buy in the very best neighborhood, so you will have to compromise on location. If you plan to pay all cash, then terms are of very little importance, but in a tight money market, attractive terms offered by the seller can add real value to the property.

All in all, the four elements should be weighed together in making a value decision. And remember, with the knowledge you now have, by the time you have finished making a thorough search of the market, you will be in a good position to make a reasonably accurate value decision.

Finally, real estate agents do not sell houses. Houses sell houses. The agent is there to understand your needs and to put knowledge of the market to work in showing you the properties that best meet those needs in the shortest possible period of time. The decision to buy is yours, and yours alone.

What Happens Next?

You have found your dream home. Now what do you do? It sounds like it is time to take a deep breath, look your agent straight in the eye, and say "Let's make an offer."

In the following discussion, which will be lengthy, I will utilize the Regional Data Service Real Estate Purchase Contract and Receipt for Deposit (Appendix B-1). This is a form with which I am very familiar and it is one of the most complete forms utilized in the industry, as far as I know.

Depending upon what part of the country you are from, the format to which you will be exposed will probably be different. That does not make it a bad format. It may not be as detailed, but it is more than likely a format that has worked in your area for some time. All of the formats can have addenda attached to them, so if you see something in the format that I will be using that you think is important, but is missing in the one that you are asked to use, then insist that it be added.

Please refer to Appendix B-1 which has been filled out for a hypothetical offer to purchase. From this point on, we will carry this transaction through the various stages of offer, counter-offer, etc., right through to the close of escrow. Therefore, it is very important that you follow along with this and the other accompanying forms in order to fully appreciate the explanations that will accompany each.

As we go through these forms, we will not just be concerned with the business of getting a legal document filled out properly, but also with the emotions involved. The forms are important, but even more important, they provide a good outline for keeping the discussion orderly.

Where the forms are physically filled out is up to you. I have filled them out in my office, in the buyer's home, on the hood of my car with the buyer holding a flashlight over my shoulder — just about anywhere. Ideally, though, some place comfortable and quiet where all parties concerned can easily participate in the proceedings is preferred.

Because you are about to make an offer to purchase a major asset involving a great deal of money, you have every right to expect a thorough and complete explanation of every word, phrase, and paragraph in the document that you will ultimately be asked to sign. If your agent is a pro, this is exactly what you will get. If you do not feel comfortable with the proceedings, then do not sign. If the agent isn't cutting it at this point, insist that he get help, either from his manager or a more experienced agent, but don't sign until you are comfortable.

A Home Buyer's Scenario

Okay, here we go. I will be the agent and the prospective buyers are Bob and Pat Moore. We have found a house at 850 Exeter Avenue in San Carlos that is on the market for $379,500. It is slightly above the Moore's budget, but the comparables that we have accumulated lead us to believe that it is also somewhat overpriced. This feeling is further reinforced by the fact that the property has been on the market for nearly two months in a market where well-priced homes are selling within weeks. We have also heard that the sellers have bought another home and are very anxious to sell and get on with their lives.

As we sit around the small table in one of our conference rooms, Bob and Pat are very quiet. I know that this will be their first home and it involves a lot of money and added responsibility. I decide not to break the silence yet, so I busy myself getting the necessary paperwork stacked up for the job at hand.

Finally, Bob says to Pat, "Well, what do you think? Do you really like it enough to go through with this?"

"I really like it a lot," Pat answers, "but it's all a little scary. Do you think we're doing the right thing?"

I keep quiet. This is something the Moores will have to work out for themselves, and when they want my opinion, they will ask for it.

Bob looks at me and asks, "What do you think, Lowell? Are we doing the right thing?" Now believe me, folks, this is not the right thing to ask most real estate agents. After all, they have been working diligently to get you to this point, and I think that you would be hard pressed to find one who would tell you he thinks you are making a mistake in going through with this purchase.

I look both of them in the eye and say, "I think so, but this is a big decision for you, and I want you to be completely comfortable with it before we go any further. Maybe we should talk it out some more. Let's consider the three criteria that we originally agreed your new home should fulfill."

"What were they?" asks Pat.

"You remember. First, it has to be a house that you like. You do like this one, don't you?"

"Oh, yes," says Pat.

"What about you, Bob?"

"I think it's great," he answers. "It's the next criterion that I'm more concerned about."

"What's that?" asks Pat.

"Whether we can afford it. This is higher then we originally intended to go."

"I know," Pat says.

Silence. Finally, I say, "Let's go over the finances as they apply to this property and be absolutely sure that you can afford it. And while we are at it, let's back into a purchase price. Is that okay with you?"

"That would really help," sighs Pat.

"Sounds good," murmurs Bob.

"Okay. As I remember, you said you had between $60,000 and $65,000 to put down, and you could not handle monthly payments greater than $3,000. Depending upon the final sale price, the taxes will be approximately $300.00 per month and the insurance should be about $100.00 per month. That leaves $2,600.00 per month for mortgage payments if you stretched it to the maximum."

"Which I really don't want to do if we can help it," Pat says.

"I understand, but we have to have some place to start."

Bob interjects, "Okay, I see what you are doing."

I check my calculator and say, "All right. $2,600.00 a month at 10% for thirty years would allow you to borrow $296,272. If we add $296,272 to the $60,000 down, that adds up to a maximum price of $356,272, and that does not take closing costs into consideration."

"Then I don't see how we can do it," Pat says gloomily.

"You can't, not if you pay full price. But we have also determined from the comps that the price is higher than the present market value."

"What do you think the present market value is?" asks Pat.

I pull out the comp sheet, study it for a minute, and lay it down for both to see. "Based on this, I would say between $358,000 and $365,000."

Pat asks, "Do you really think that they will go down that much?" She begins to look a little more hopeful.

"They will if they want to sell it," I reply. "I wouldn't pay any more than that. And remember, they have bought another house, so they are going to have to get realistic about the price pretty soon. Why not right now with your offer?"

"I agree," says Bob. "So we make an offer. If they take it, great. If they don't, we haven't lost anything." He has now come to grips with the situation. He looks at Pat. "Okay with you, honey?"

"I really would like to have it. I hope they will accept our offer."

Bob turns to me. "Let's write it up. Since their asking price is quite a lot higher than what we are willing to pay, I think I would prefer to offer pretty close to my best price and hold firm. Also, since I am assured of very significant increases in earnings over the next few years, I would like to ask the owners to take back a small second interest — for five years maybe. Do you think they would go for that?"

"Don't know. But it can't hurt to try. What price do you want to offer?"

"I don't know. What about $355,000." He looks at Pat. "What do you think, hon?"

"I was thinking more. Lowell, what do you think?"

"It sounds like a good place to start. I'm not sure that it will fly, but I doubt that it will die at that price. Let's give it a try."

This is a very natural discourse of putting together an offer and would be carried on throughout the entire process. Let's look at the offer format now in detail.

4
The Purchase Contract

On the purchase contract (Appendix B-1) the heading describes where the contract is being filled out (Menlo Park), the date (essential to any contract), the parties making the offer (Robert C. & Patricia H. Moore, Husband & Wife), the offering price ($355,000.00), and the complete address of the property including City (San Carlos), County (San Mateo), State (California), and description (850 Exeter Avenue).

Particularly in states with community property laws, it is a good idea to list the marital status of the buyers after their names, because very often what is written down here finds its way undisturbed all the way to the recorded deed. Bob and Pat could have been brother and sister. If that were the case and Bob was married and Pat was single, the names should read, "Robert C. Moore, a married man and Patricia H. Moore, a single woman." Just be sure that you are described as you really are.

Under property description, a street address will usually suffice, provided the property has a street address. In rural areas, this may not be true. In that case, some description that uniquely describes the property will be required.

PROPERTY DESCRIPTION

In addition to a street address, a property also has a legal description. Legal descriptions exist in one of the following three forms: 1) Recorded Tract, Map, Lot and Block System, 2) U.S. Government Section and Township System, and 3) Metes and Bounds System.

In most urban areas, the county tax assessor will have set up a system of maps covering the entire area. The maps will be divided into blocks and the blocks further divided into lots. The map, block, and lot number make up the parcel number, a unique number in that county for that particular property. Armed with the parcel number and access to the county records, it is easy to locate any property on the county maps. These records are kept in the county recorder's office. Many real estate firms subscribe to a service which provides a microfiche copy of the county records. They update the microfiche on a regular basis.

In rural areas where you are dealing with large parcels of land, the Section and Township System is used. An in-depth explanation of this system would be too cumbersome, however, a brief description is in order. The government has divided the country with principal meridians (lines running north and south) and base lines (lines running east and west). Between the principal meridians, every six miles is a range line. Between the base lines, every six miles is a township line. These range and township lines make up a patchwork of squares called township squares, which measure six miles by six miles. The township squares are divided into thirty-six one mile square sections. The sections are further divided into quarters, and the quarters are divided into quarters, and on and on. A numbering system is utilized, referenced from the principal meridian and base line so that even the smallest division of property will have a unique description.

The Metes and Bounds System utilizes measured distances, compass point directions, and natural monuments. In the past, it would not be unusual for a description of a property line to read, "from the lone oak tree to the center of Sutters Creek." This is great until someone cuts down the oak tree or the creek dries up. Metes and bounds legal descriptions are still provided on a regular basis by surveyors, however, monuments (trees, boulders, barns, etc.) are no longer used. Most people find such descriptions very difficult to read, but if this is the way your property is described, then it is important to be sure that the description properly describes the property that you think you are buying.

Back to the purchase contract.

FINANCING TERMS

The first section of the Real Estate Purchase Contract covers the financial aspects of the offer. The offering price is $355,000. Because Robert has been with his present company less than a year and cannot show a past history of earnings that would substantiate his present or future earnings potential, we decide to go for a 75% easy qualifier first in the amount of $266,250 and ask the seller to take

back an interest only second in the amount of $35,000.

The total cash investment is $53,750 ($2,000 Deposit + $8,650 upon satisfaction of all contingencies + $43,100 at time of closing) plus closing costs. The closing costs will be approximately $8,375 (2% of $266,250 = $5,375 + approximately 1% of $355,000 = $3,550), resulting in a total cash requirement of $62,125. Total monthly payments will be approximately $2,734.73 ($2047.23 principal and interest on first + $291.67 interest on second + $295.83 property taxes + $100.00 homeowner's insurance). These figures fit within the Moore's limits.

In making this offer we are stating that the additional deposit of $8,650.00 will be forthcoming as soon as all of the contingencies are satisfied and removed. The dates for removing these contingencies are covered later.

Please note that the total deposit of $10,650 ($2,000 + $8,650) equals 3% of the purchase price. This ties into the liquidated damages clause which will be discussed later. Also, a personal check is fine for these initial deposits but the balance of cash at closing will have to be in the form of a cashier's check or a bank transfer.

Paragraph 1(H) is designed to force the buyer to apply for financing in a timely fashion. This protects the seller from having his property held off of the market by a buyer who either may not be totally serious about purchasing or may not be qualified to purchase. Many lending institutions can rule on a potential purchaser's credit-worthiness in seventy-two hours or less. Therefore, the sooner we get an application made, the sooner we will know if the transaction is going to hold together from a credit standpoint.

Paragraph 1(I) gets us into the actual mortgage contingency. This paragraph makes this contract contingent upon the buyers being successful at obtaining a loan under the terms and conditions stated in paragraph 1(D). This is why the terms and conditions of the loan are spelled out so explicitly in 1(D). The buyers do not just want a loan for $266,250. They want it to be for thirty years at an interest rate not to exceed 8.5% with payments of $2,047.23 per month. Furthermore, they want the total cap of the loan to be no more than 13.5% and the points not to exceed 2%.

If any of these conditions cannot be met, then the buyers have the option to nullify the contract. The time limits for this and other contingencies are spelled out in Section 8. It is important that this and all contingencies either be removed or extended within the time limit prescribed by the contract or you will be technically out of contract.

Because the buyer can walk away from the contract at no cost based upon this contingency, the terms have to be reasonably obtainable or no well-informed seller would be willing to consider the offer. The terms set forth here do not preclude the buyer from trying to obtain better terms than stated. The idea is to make the contract contingent upon reasonable terms that will be acceptable to everyone, and then go out and shop for the very best loan available.

Paragraph 1(J) deals with the assumption of the seller's mortgage. This paragraph requires the seller to provide the buyer within a specified period of time all pertinent information regarding the loan to be assumed, and gives the buyer a specified period of time to accept or reject in writing these terms and conditions. This is not applicable in our example, but would be a contingency if an assumption were involved.

An impound account is set up by the lender when the lender collects a pro rata portion of the taxes and insurance costs each month along with the regular monthly mortgage payment. The lender then pays these bills directly when they come due. Many lenders insist upon providing this service to be absolutely sure that the taxes and insurance are always paid on time. After all, a tax lien would

precede the bank's lien on the property, and if the house burned down and the insurance had not been paid, the bank's security would have just gone up in smoke. The greater the down payment, the less the lender will worry about an impound account. The last paragraph in 1(J) is simply saying that an existing impound account will be transferred from seller to buyer without penalty or benefit to either party. In our example, this paragraph is not applicable.

REAL PROPERTY AND PERSONAL PROPERTY

Section 2 distinguishes fixtures, which are considered real property, from personal property. Real estate, or real property, is the land and anything permanently attached to it. Paragraph 2(A) covers the fixtures (real property) which are always included as a part of the transaction unless specifically excluded. A dining room chandelier is often such an exclusion. Paragraph 2(B) covers personal property. In this example, we asked that the refrigerator, washer, and dryer be included in the sale. Here in our area, window coverings, including the draperies, are considered as being included unless otherwise stated. This may not be the case everywhere.

CONDITIONS RELATING TO TITLE

Paragraph 3 deals with title. Paragraph 3(A) requires that the seller provide to the buyer within a specified period all documentation relating to title. This includes the Covenants, Conditions, and Restrictions (CC&R's) in the case of condominiums or subdivisions governed by such, and Homeowner's Association Bylaws, Rules, and Regulations if such an association exists. The buyer then has a specified period of time to approve the information provided.

Paragraph 3(B) deals with bonds and assessments which are usually repaid over a long period, typically fifteen years, and are very often included as a part of the tax bill. The obligation is usually assumed by the buyer.

Some assessments are short term in nature and require one substantial lump sum payment. In this case, the buyer might understandably not be willing to assume such an obligation and expect it to be paid off prior to taking title.

In any event, the buyer certainly has the right to know and approve that which he is being asked to assume. In this contract form, this is being treated as one more contingency which needs to be removed in writing. (See section 8.)

Paragraph 3(C) states that the seller must deliver to the buyer a marketable title, free and clear of encumbrances, restrictions, etc., with certain exceptions. It states who pays for the title insurance (in this case, the buyer), the company who will provide the title insurance (First American Title), and who will pay the escrow fee (the buyer). In other areas this will be different depending upon local custom, and in any case this can be a matter of negotiation.

Paragraph 3(D) deals with risk of loss and states that any loss occurring before transfer of title will be borne solely by the seller, and any expenditures made by the buyer to this point will be reimbursed by the seller and the contract is null and void, except that the buyer has the option to either maintain the contract in force or attempt to renegotiate the contract based upon a diminished value resulting from the loss.

Paragraph 3(E) is probably unique to California. Because of Proposition 13, property is taxed at 1% of the purchase price, so every time a property changes hands, the tax also changes. There may be other states that reevaluate upon change of ownership, but in most states a reevaluation will take place for the entire area (town) every so many years. However, the assessments will change annu-

ally depending upon the local government's budget for that year.

SPECIAL ADDENDA

It is often necessary to attach special addenda to a standard contract to purchase. This section allows for the acknowledgment of the attachment of such addenda and ties the addenda to the contract. In this example, there will be a Finance Addendum attached which will cover the specific terms of the seller (second mortgage) carryback. This will be discussed at the end of the purchase contract.

BUYER BEWARE OR SELLER BEWARE?

Section 5 deals with a seller's transfer disclosure, mandated by California law to be provided in every real estate transaction involving one to four residential units, effective January 1, 1987. This law requires that all sellers, except executors of estates who have no knowledge of the property, provide a full disclosure concerning the property on a prescribed form. This requirement holds regardless of whether or not a real estate agent is involved.

As I grew up in real estate, the Latin term *caveat emptor,* meaning "buyer beware," kept coming up time and again. I suspect that in many parts of the country, the buyer is still pretty much on his own in looking out for his best interests. Not so in California. An attitude of consumer protectionism, a number of court decisions, and some recently revised real estate laws have turned things nearly one hundred eighty degrees to where we now say seller beware. To comply with the law and to protect both the sellers and the agents from future lawsuits, full disclosure has become the order of the day.

There are several potential results of this requirement. First, if the seller does not provide the disclosure, then the buyer can walk away from the transaction any time he so desires with no penalty.

If the seller provides false information, then he is setting himself up for a potential lawsuit with the evidence stacked against him in his own handwriting. This is not a requirement to be taken lightly.

Paragraph 5(B) specifically states that the seller is required by California law to disclose the fact if any additions or alterations have been made without a proper building permit. This is redundant to the disclosure statement itself, but serves as a reminder that the law is very specific on this point.

MANDATED DISCLOSURES

Paragraph A: Because California is subject to earthquakes, special study zones have been set up and must be disclosed. This can be accomplished with a $40.00 report that can be ordered by phone.

Paragraph B: Flood hazard zones have also been established and must be disclosed.

Paragraph C: The Enabling Declaration, by-laws, etc. must be provided in the sale of any condominium/PUD.

Paragraph D: Smoke detectors are required by law when a property changes ownership.

Paragraph E: If the seller carries any or all of the financing, then a financing disclosure statement is required.

Paragraph F: Real estate buyers have now been pressed into service as unpaid agents of the IRS. Read the paragraph; it's interesting. The gist is this: Uncle Sam has been getting stiffed on capital gains taxes from a lot of foreigners who have sold properties in the United States, retreated to their native land, and then told the IRS to take a hike. The Foreign Investment in Real Property Tax Act requires a buyer to withhold 10% of the gross sales on behalf of the IRS if the seller is a "foreign person." Failure to comply could result in the buyer

and/or the agents involved being liable for this tax if the IRS is unsuccessful in collecting from the seller. It is extremely important to get this form filled out or to be sure that the funds are held in escrow, whichever is appropriate.

Paragraph G: An Energy Audit and Compliance form is required in some areas.

Paragraph H: This provides a blank line for any additional disclosures that we haven't thought of yet.

TIME IS OF THE ESSENCE

Section 7 — Time Is Of The Essence, is essential to any legal contract if dates are to be strictly adhered to. Obviously, people cannot afford to close on approximately such-and-such date. They usually need to know precisely.

CONTINGENCY REMOVALS

Section 8 deals with the removal of the various contingencies found throughout the contract. It is most important that everyone understands the impact of contingency removal.

It should be explicitly understood that if a contingency is not removed or extended within the specified time limit, then in accordance with the terms of this contract, at the option of the seller the contract is null and void.

Many people are under the mistaken opinion that if a contingency is not removed in a timely fashion, then the rights attached to that contingency are lost, and the contract is still in effect. This may actually be true in some areas, so it is extremely important to understand precisely what your contract really says.

This particular contract form is set up so the financing contingency — 8(A) — is removed and separated from the myriad of other contingencies. The rationale here is that the seller will insist upon the removal of the contingencies grouped under Paragraph 8(A) as quickly as possible, while the financing contingency may realistically take thirty days or longer.

In our example, we have a thirty-day financing contingency and fourteen days to remove all of the other contingencies. Since the credit-worthiness of the buyer can be checked out well within the fourteen days, the seller should know whether or not he has a deal within two weeks.

Because we are offering a low price and asking for owner financing, we want the rest of the contract to be as palatable to the seller as possible.

It should be noted that the various contingencies listed in Paragraph 8(A) could be removed at various times, but as long as any one remains in force, the contract is tenuous; therefore, it is simpler and involves less paperwork to remove them all at once. One caution: the time limit must be sufficient to cover the contingency that will take the longest to remove. Be sure to look at Appendix B-3: Contingency Removal Schedule and Appendix B-4: Contingency Release Clause Addendum.

HOME PROTECTION PLANS

Home Protection Plans are covered by section 9 and are available from a number of companies which provide a limited warranty on appliances, heaters, water heaters, etc., for a cost of between $200.00 and $500.00, depending upon the size of the property and the equipment to be covered. These plans can be put into effect with a simple phone call, so you can imagine that there are a fair number of exceptions to the coverage. Generally speaking, I do not go out of my way recommending these plans, but I must admit that on occasion I hear of someone who makes out very well as a result of having had one. By initialing Paragraph 9(A), it is agreed that no plan will be utilized. Paragraph 9(B) is utilized to specify the Home Protec-

tion Plan company, the price, and how this is to be paid.

LIQUIDATED DAMAGES ACCORDING TO STATE LAW

As we discuss this subject, please remember that the discussion is based upon California law, and the law may be different in your area. Paragraph 10(A) addresses two points of law.

First, if the paragraph is not initialed by BOTH the buyer and seller, then in the case of a default by the buyer, the seller shall be released from his obligation to sell the property to the buyer and may proceed against the buyer through the normal legal system. It is generally conceded that the real winners in this course of action are the lawyers. If the paragraph is initialed by both parties, then the deposit may be retained by the seller in the case of a default by the buyer.

The second aspect of this paragraph has to do with whether or not the buyer intends to occupy the property as his residence, and whether or not the property consists of four or fewer residential units. If both criteria are true, then California law restricts liquidated damages to no more than 3% of the purchase price.

Since the paragraph reads that the liquidated damages will be the amount of the deposit or 3% of the purchase price, whichever is less, it is understandable for the seller to insist that the deposit be at least 3% of the purchase price.

It should be completely understood that this paragraph only becomes effective if the buyer defaults. A default is quite different from the failure to remove a contingency. If the purchase agreement is contingent upon the buyer securing acceptable financing and the buyer cannot, then the purchase agreement is null and void and all funds are returned. However, due diligence in attempting to secure the financing is required.

If the buyer is suddenly transferred to a new job out of the area or simply gets cold feet, then the seller is entitled to liquidated damages.

Paragraph 10(B) answers the question as to whether or not the purchaser intends to occupy the premises as his residence.

Paragraph 10(C) simply states that all parties agree to execute a "Receipt For Increased Deposit" at the time of any increase in deposit. This receipt reiterates the terms of Paragraph 10(A).

STRUCTURAL PEST CONTROL CERTIFICATION

Section 11 deals with a structural pest control certification and should be applicable in most parts of the country. Paragraph 11(A) determines who will provide and pay for the report and sets a time limit for doing so. It should be understood that whomever pays for the report also gets to choose the company making the report. Most pest control companies not only provide a report, but also bid on making the corrections; it should be relatively obvious that a potential conflict of interest exists.

The requirement for a clean structural pest control certification has been a real boon to the contractors in this business. Since most lending institutions will not fund without a certification, the property cannot be sold without it. It is my opinion that there has been widespread abuse in this area, and the real estate community is constantly trading notes trying to sort out the abusers from the fair and honest contractors.

The point is, the buyer wants to buy a property free of infestation and infection, but not at an expense to either the buyer or the seller for overpriced work or work that is simply not required.

Partly because of past abuses and partly because it is superior from a marketing point of view, most sellers are now ordering the pest control report as soon as they list the property for sale. This way

they feel that they have more control, and they know where they stand as far as potential expenses go before they have an offer in hand. This way, they have time to get second or even third opinions, and if the work required to correct the problems is excessive, they can attempt to negotiate the cost in a counter-offer to the prospective buyer.

Paragraph 11(B) states that if the report indicates no problems, then the certification will be issued along with the report.

Paragraph 11(C) states that the work will be paid for by the seller and that the funds will be held in escrow until the certification or clearance is issued. This is probably a good time to mention that the pest control report is not just concerned with insects (termites, etc.). It is also concerned with dry rot and fungus, usually caused by wood members in enclosed areas being subjected to moisture. Very often, a pest control report will require the repair of leaking plumbing or bathtub tile as part of the corrective measure. If it is an insect, it is referred to as infestation. If it is dry rot or fungus, it is referred to as infection.

Pest control reports usually contain two separate types of conditions. The first type is a pre-existing condition, which is basically what we have been talking about. It is the responsibility of the seller, at least the way this particular contract is set up.

The second type includes things that are likely to lead to a problem and are NOT the responsibility of the seller. An example would be debris in the crawl space. These items can be completed at the buyer's option and expense. This is covered by Paragraph 11(D).

Paragraph 11(E) deals with inaccessible areas. If the report recommends that certain inaccessible areas be explored, then the buyer has an interesting choice. He may opt not to incur the expense of the additional inspection; however, many lending institutions will not go along with this. If he does authorize the additional inspection and no damage or sign of infestation is found, then the total expense is his. If damage or infestation is found, then the expense of all corrective action, including the opening and closing of the area, shall be borne by the seller.

LEGAL NATURE OF THE AGREEMENT

Paragraph 12(A) states that this writing is the entire agreement. This is true; however, a counteroffer referencing this document will make it a part of a new agreement. Paragraph 12(B) states that this is a binding agreement and that the buyer cannot assign his rights without the prior consent of the seller.

Paragraph 12(C) deals with the rules of arbitration in the event of a dispute over the disposition of the deposit. Paragraph 12(D) is a standard statement as to who pays any attorney's fees incurred. Paragraph 12(E) provides authorization to the broker to disseminate information, usually through the MLS, concerning price and terms of the sale. This can only be disseminated after close of escrow. There might be an occasion when you would not want some part of this information to be made public. The time to object is now.

CONDITION OF PROPERTY

Section 13 represents a new and quite revolutionary way of thinking in residential real estate transactions, as it provides the buyer with the opportunity to contract with licensed contractors or other qualified professionals to thoroughly inspect and provide him with an opinion as to the condition of the property. If he is not satisfied with the findings, then he can cancel the contract and is entitled to a full refund of his deposit.

This provision, along with the Transfer Disclosure Statement (to be discussed later), may still be unique to California, however, it is only a matter of time before this inspection opportunity is strongly endorsed by realtors all across the country.

If such a paragraph does not exist in the contracts customarily used in your area, I highly recommend that you insist upon including an addendum which will provide to you the same rights of a complete inspection and report by trade professionals as is provided in this paragraph.

Insisting on this provision in your contract could potentially save you untold grief, not to mention a great deal of money. Remember, *caveat emptor* — buyer beware.

Paragraph 13(A) creates the contingency. This provides the buyer with all of the rights of inspection to be completed within the time limits specified under Paragraph 8(B).

There is another aspect to this paragraph which states that the buyer must provide to the seller a written copy of any inspector's reports. This was included in an attempt to prevent the buyer from cancelling for unfounded reasons. However, in this era of full disclosure, it has actually placed an additional burden upon the seller. Once in receipt of such reports, the seller is then obligated to make future buyers aware of their contents. This could certainly make it very difficult for the seller to disclaim knowledge of defects that have been so documented. It is definitely recommended that the buyer not waive this right of inspection. It is also strongly recommended that the buyer not abuse this right.

It should be fairly obvious in reality that the buyer could use this particular contingency to cancel the contract for practically any reason, including just plain cold feet. For this reason, the seller will usually insist that the time to remove this contingency be as short as practical, since the property has effectively been removed from the market during this contingency period with no real assurance that it will result in a sale.

It should also be fairly obvious that this contingency will occasionally open the whole contract for renegotiation as a result of the bringing to light of hidden defects. Since such defects could have a profound effect on value, this is as it should be.

Finally, please note that Paragraph 13(A) provides that the buyer holds harmless the brokers, agents, and the seller for any costs and/or damages incurred as a result of these inspections. This is also as it should be.

Paragraph 13(B) simply states that the buyer is aware of the approximate age of the house and should not expect it to meet the same standards as a new house. This is nice, but I doubt that it has any legal impact on the contract.

Paragraph 13(C) is a disclaimer concerning square footage. This paragraph stems from sellers and/or agents providing erroneous information about square footage. They nearly always err on the high side. If the buyer is sensitive to square footage, then he should get out there and measure rather than rely upon someone else's assertion. That is why this disclaimer has been included in this section.

MAINTENANCE OF HOUSE

Section 14 has to do with all aspects of the property being maintained in good working order between the date of the contract and the time of closing and transfer of possession.

This is a very important section and should be included in any contract to purchase. A walk-through just prior to closing should be made to ascertain that the conditions of this paragraph have been met. If they have not, them some provision should be made before closing is completed to rectify the situation.

This is just one of those eleventh hour situations that can quickly become a nightmare if not handled properly. It is not at all uncommon to find windows broken, appliances not working, and all

manner of problems. If the problems are really major, you may not wish to close at all, however, at such a late date, you may have very little choice.

The usual solution in these cases is to have an adequate sum held in escrow out of the seller's proceeds as assurance that the problems will be fixed or otherwise rectified.

KEYS

Section 15 requires little explanation. It has been included for good reason. More than one home has been purchased and escrow closed, and then the buyer has had to break into his new possession because no one remembered to provide keys and the seller is long gone. It is highly recommended that the locks be re-keyed for security.

DUAL AGENCY AND DISCLOSURE

As stated before, there exists a conflict between the letter of the law and accepted practice, causing the real estate broker a serious dilemma. The best solution to this problem is full disclosure, and that is what this section is all about.

Dual agency exists when one agent represents both the buyer and the seller. If Mary Jones of Smith Realty represents the seller and Bill Roberts of Roberts Realty represents the buyer, there is no problem of dual agency. If Mary Jones represents both buyer and seller, then it is obvious that Mary Jones and Smith Realty are operating in the capacity of dual agent. What may not be as obvious is a situation where Mary Jones of Smith Realty represents the seller and Carol White, also of Smith Realty, represents the buyer. This is a dual agency, because only the broker, Smith Realty, has a direct agency and fiduciary relationship with the principal, and Mary Jones and Carol White both work for this same agency.

It is difficult but possible for an agent to work in a dual agency capacity and still do a good job for all parties concerned. The first thing that the agent must do is inform both sides that his role has now become one of messenger and mediator, but he cannot disclose confidences given by either party.

The confidences of greatest concern here have to do with price and terms. In such a situation, the seller should not disclose his bottom price nor should the buyer disclose his top price. The problem, as I see it, is that the seller may well have disclosed certain confidences to the agent long before the dual agency situation ever arose. When this is the case, the agent must exercise a great deal of discretion in order not to violate those confidences. Appendix B-5 is the form used by the California Association of Realtors: Disclosure Regarding Real Estate Agency Relationships.

OTHER TERMS AND CONDITIONS

Section 17 provides some blank lines for other terms and conditions not found in the body of this form. This is where you could write in making this sale contingent upon the sale of another property. Very often, the buyers cannot purchase one property without the sale of their present home. Normally, such a contingency is set up on a seventy-two-hour release clause.

This means that the seller accepts the offer with the understanding that his property will continue to be marketed. If a second buyer is secured, then the original buyer has seventy-two hours to remove this contingency, or the contract is null and void and the second buyer takes over.

There are all kinds of contingencies that can be written in here, such as special financing terms or the ability to obtain a building permit.

If there is not enough space for whatever needs to be written, then just use the space to refer to a separate addendum.

ESCROW CONDITIONS AND INSTRUCTIONS

Before we get into Section 18, we should take a minute to be sure the role of an escrow company is understood.

An escrow is created by mutual consent between the two parties to a contract (in our case between buyer and seller) with a third party, who holds an equal fiduciary responsibility to each party.

This third party, or escrow officer and/or company, is bound by the mutually agreed upon terms of the buyer and seller. These should always be in writing. In our case, this mutual agreement includes the original purchase contract, its counter offers, and any addendum thereto. The escrow company is charged with accepting funds into a trust account for the particular transaction, and then making sure that all of the agreed upon terms and conditions are met before releasing these funds.

Specifically, the initial deposit, all additional increases in deposit, the proceeds from mortgages or deeds of trust, and any additional cash required to complete the transaction, are all placed into the tender loving care of the escrow company.

It is then the escrow company's responsibility to see that all of the terms of the agreement are fully satisfied. This includes, but is not limited to, the removal of all contingencies and the providing of a good and marketable title.

When all of the funds are in place and all other terms and conditions have been met, then title is recorded in the name(s) of the new owner(s) and the proceeds of the closing are released to the seller. This point in time is referred to as the close of escrow. Unless special arrangements to the contrary have been agreed upon in advance, this is also when possession changes.

In California and many other states, the title companies also serve as the escrow companies, and handle the vast majority of the escrows. Escrows can also be handled by real estate brokers and attorneys.

Section 18(A) sets the date for close of escrow. In the case of our example, we set a date approximately sixty days from now, realizing that we could easily close in forty-five days or less, but holding this as a negotiating point if needed later on.

Paragraph 18(B) determines when physical possession will change hands. To avoid potential problems, possession should be as simultaneous with the close of escrow as possible. This rule is often broken, but the risk to the party giving possession could be great.

For the seller who allows early possession, there is always the risk that the buyer will not perform at closing and also refuse to move. It could cost a great deal in time and money before the seller retrieves possession of his property. Then he has to start all over again marketing his property.

For the buyer who allows the seller to stay on beyond the closing date, it is always possible that he will stay on long beyond the agreed upon vacancy date. This, then, becomes a major inconvenience as well as a costly problem for the buyer.

If it becomes absolutely imperative that the non-owner be in possession for any period of time whatsoever, then a written agreement should be executed before such possession takes place. This agreement should include a per diem rent and an absolute date when such possession will cease. It is a good idea to include in the agreement a severe penalty should this date be missed.

Paragraph 18(C) deals with the proration of taxes, rents, insurance, etc. These items should be prorated as of the date of closing.

Paragraph 18(D) deals with who pays the property transfer taxes. It is just about universal across the country that county transfer taxes are assessed at the rate of $1.10 per each $1,000.00 or portion thereof of the sale price. Some areas may have a city transfer tax on top of this.

Paragraph 18(E) states that funds will not be released from escrow without the signatures of all parties to the contract, including the broker's.

Paragraph 18(F) is essentially a hold harmless clause for the escrow company.

OFFER AND ACCEPTANCE

Paragraph 19(A) provides for a date and time, beyond which the offer is deemed revoked unless accepted by the seller. This is also where everybody gets to sign and date the offer. Paragraph 19(B) spells out the brokerage fee. Paragraph 19(C), when initialled by the seller, indicates that the offer is accepted subject to a counter-offer. It is very important, from the seller's point of view, that he not fail to initial here. Otherwise, he could intend to make a counter-offer, but there would be nothing to tie it into the signed acceptance of this offer. Paragraph 19(D) is the acceptance statement below which comes the seller's signature and date of signing. In addition to the signatures on this last page, all other pages should be initialled by all parties concerned.

One final word about the offer. Any offer, whether it is the initial offer, as this is, or a counter offer, can be withdrawn at any time prior to it being accepted. It is important to keep this in mind. Situations are constantly arising where it is important to understand this fact of contract law.

FINANCING ADDENDUM

If you are not too weary to remember back to the beginning of the contract, you will recall that one of the provisions was that the seller would take back a second mortgage; therefore, we need to fill out a Financing Addendum (Appendix B-2).

If you review this form, you can see that it is primarily designed for the benefit of the seller, and acts as additional instructions to the escrow agent.

Since this was checked off as being a part of the contract way back in section 4, we will go through this quickly at this time. Even though this is for the benefit of the seller and would ultimately be the responsibility of the seller's agent to prepare and make a part of the contract, there is a good psychological reason for the buyer's agent to prepare this with the original contract.

You are asking the seller to take back financing, which he probably does not want to do; the least you can do is to show him that you are approaching the request in a professional manner, and that you are offering all of the provisions and safeguards that are customary no matter who the lender might be. As I said before, ask for the things that are really important to you, then make the rest of the contract as palatable as possible to the seller.

There are seven sections to this Financing Addendum, and each one, initialled by both buyer(s) and seller(s), will become a part of the contract.

Section 1 allows for an Acceleration and/or Due on Sale Clause. This means that in the event of buyer's default or the sale of the property, the note is due and payable in full.

Section 2 instructs the escrow agent to have recorded a Request for Notice of Default. It is only natural that the seller would want to know if adverse things are happening to his collateral.

Section 3 provides the seller with the opportunity to check and either approve or disapprove buyer's credit within the time limit specified in the contract.

Section 4 provides for a late charge if periodic payment is more than ten days late.

Section 5 specifies that buyer will maintain Fire & Extended Coverage Insurance and name the seller as loss payee.

Section 6 specifies that a property tax service will be utilized. If you recall, such a service will collect the taxes (and sometimes the insurance premium) monthly and then pay the necessary items when due. This is offered to protect the position of the lenders. I do not recommend this service to any responsible buyer since the funds are tied well in advance of the due dates and generally no interest is paid.

Section 7 provides for a Balloon Payment. Going back to the terms of the contract, the Moores have asked the seller to take back a second mortgage in the amount of $35,000 at 10% interest only for five years. This means that during those five years the Moores will be paying only interest on the loan, and the entire $35,000 will be due and payable at the end of the five years. This is called a balloon payment. Before entering into such a financing arrangement, both the buyer and seller should have a reasonably clear-cut idea of where the money is going to come from to pay the lump sum principal balance when due.

Going through the contract and addendum may be tedious, but it is necessary to provide insights into various aspects of the residential real estate transaction so that you, as buyer or seller, know exactly what you're doing.

5
The Sale at Last

PRESENTING THE OFFER: THE AGENT'S ROLE

Now we can look carefully at the agent's role in presenting the offer. The agent now becomes the emissary of the buyer, and in this role he can be very useful and effective, although he clearly has no power to make decisions and can do little more than advise, explain his client's position, and carry messages back and forth.

The first step for the buyer's agent is to call the seller's agent and arrange an appointment to meet with the seller and the seller's agent. The buyers will not be included in this meeting.

The meeting is set for 8:00 P.M. that evening at the seller's house. As the buyer's agent, I would be sure to be right on time — not late, not early. With any luck, the seller's agent is already there.

After introductions all around, it is up to me to present my offer. I will start by telling them about the buyers — where they work, information about their family, their present housing situation, any other information that would affect their ability to perform (positive information, we hope), and finally, a few of the things they particularly like about the house.

Next, I will produce comparables that will support the price that I am about to offer. This often creates quite a discussion. That's just fine. Better to get this out of the way before they have even seen the offer. By the time this discussion is over, they just know that it is not going to be a full price offer; what they don't know is just how bad it is going to be.

Next, I bring out all of the good features of the offer in general terms without actually opening up the offer. In this particular case, I would point out that the buyers have no house to sell in order to purchase this one. I would further point out that they are renting on a month-to-month basis and are willing to close just as soon as a bank will fund. I emphasize these points because I know that the sellers have already bought another home and a rapid close is becoming very important. I do not mention their dilemma because I do not want them to feel as if I am trying to intimidate them into accepting this offer. They are well aware of their situation.

Now it is time to present the offer. Almost all knowledgeable agents agree that once the seller has been made aware of the offered price, he will probably pay very little attention to anything else, especially if the offered price is well below his expectations. This is why I try to get all of the positive aspects of the offer into the seller's mind in the preliminary discussion, since the price will be staring the seller right in the face once I present a copy of the offer to all parties concerned.

At this point, I will say something like, "As you can see, the offer is for $355,000." At the same time, I watch the sellers very carefully for their reactions. If they have a professional agent, they have been told to listen politely to everything I have to say, but not to comment or react. If they have been given this advice and follow it, I will probably learn very little at this point.

All agents are not created equal and not all sellers can restrain themselves. I have seen emotions from mild disappointment to outright rage to utter despair. The emotion registered here is often a very valuable clue as to the course and strategy for future negotiations.

Let's assume that in this case the husband expresses some mild anger, and at the same time I note a hint of despair in his wife's expression. Let's also assume that their agent intercedes at this point (the proper thing to do), and suggests that they worry about the price later and that we go over the rest of the contract. Everyone agrees (although we know that the price continues to lurk close to the forefront of their minds), and I proceed to go through the contract in its entirety, again emphasizing the positive aspects (from the seller's point of view) as I come upon them.

In this particular case I would try to turn the request for the owners to carry back a small second mortgage into a positive, pointing out that this allows the buyers to go for an easy qualifier (75% or less) first mortgage.

Finally, when I am finished, I come back to the price one last time. I might say something like, "I know you are a little disappointed with the price of this offer, but I must point out two things that

you should know before you make a decision concerning the price. First, my buyers are quite close to their maximum capabilities price-wise; and second, they feel that they have made a very good offer based not only on their own capabilities, but on what the comparables say the market value for your property really is. No matter what any of us feel or desire, it really is the market that sets the value, isn't it?"

At this point, I would most likely be told that they would like to discuss the offer privately. Most agents would push for a quick answer by suggesting that they wait outside or somewhere out of earshot, rather than simply drive away without at least a counter-offer. I subscribe to this theory except when it becomes obvious that forcing a quick decision will most likely produce a decision that is not in my client's best interest.

In this particular case, I know that the sellers are extremely motivated to consummate a sale, what with the prospect of being the proud owners of two homes somewhere in the not-too-distant future. So I wait outside.

After about a half hour, the other agent calls me back in, informing me that they have prepared a counter-offer.

COUNTER-OFFER

The counter-offer consists of three items:

1) The price has been countered at $365,000, but the counter has not addressed where the additional $10,000 is to come from;

2) The close of escrow has been reduced from sixty days to forty-five days;

3) The washer and dryer are not to be included in the contract.

I gather up my copies of the signed offer (now subject to the counter-offer) along with the counter-offer. I thank everyone for their time and promise to get back to them just as soon as I have had a chance to discuss the counter-offer with my clients. I leave.

Right away, I call the buyers, Bob and Pat Moore, and inform them that we have a counter-offer to consider. Naturally, they want to know all about it, and I suggest that I come right to their home so we can go over it in detail.

Soon we are seated around their dining room table and I lay out the counter-offer. They are both dismayed over the $10,000 increase in purchase price. There next ensues a good deal of conversation about how they cannot afford to pay any more than they offered, that they thought they had made a really fair offer, and on and on.

Finally, when both Bob and Pat cannot think of anything else to say, I have an opportunity to steer the conversation in a more positive direction. I suggest that they really are not all that far apart, and that they have a number of options relative to the counter-offer.

Their two obvious options are either to accept the counter as it stands or to reject it outright. I feel that neither of these is necessarily in their best interests, but that a middle road must exist that will satisfy all parties concerned. Then I suggest that we take the counter one item at a time, leaving the problem of price until last.

We quickly agree that the forty-five day close of escrow is no problem. We are glad that we had the foresight to ask for sixty days, thus providing us with a valuable bargaining chip.

Pat is not as immediately agreeable about the washer and dryer, but when I point out that they are nearly seven years old, she realizes that they really do not count for much in the overall picture. We finally agree that the washer and dryer can be excluded.

When we get to the price, Pat suggests that since they have given in on the close of escrow and the washer and dryer, the seller should give in on the price. Bob is more realistic in feeling that the seller will not accept any change in the price, but at the same time feels squeezed by the prospect of either having to increase the down payment or the first mortgage.

Here I point out that the counter-offer does not address the problem of where the additional funds are to come from. Then I suggest the following: counter the counter at $360,000, meeting them halfway. However, instead of increasing the down payment or the amount of the first mortgage, increase the second mortgage being taken back by the sellers. The impact would be as follows: for the next five years (remember, interest only for five years with one balloon payment at the end) the monthly interest payment would be increased by $41.67 and the balloon payment at the end of five years would be $40,000 instead of $35,000. With the upward mobility of Bob's earning power, neither presents a problem.

The final counter-offer to the first counter-offer to the original contract is accepted, and now the real work begins.

CONTINGENCIES OF THE CONTRACT

Under the terms of this contract, the buyers have six contingencies which must be removed in order for the contract to remain valid. I must state once again that unless the contingencies are removed in writing within the time frame specified, the contract is null and void. This is the way this particular contract is written. It is quite possible that in some areas, the contracts are written in such a way that if the holder of the contingency wants to void the contract as a result of the contingency, he must do so in writing, otherwise the contingency is lost and the contract is in full force.

Such a contract form is sneaky, at the very least, but probably legal. So beware. All contracts are not the same, and many are written to benefit one party at the expense of the other.

The contingencies in this contract are:

Financing Contingency
Preliminary Title Report
Transfer Disclosure Statement
Geological Hazards
Seller Financing Disclosure Statement
Condition Of Property

The financing contingency must be removed within thirty days. All of the rest must be removed within fourteen days.

It should be emphasized that time goes by quickly and there is very little time to waste. If undue delays are encountered and a contingency cannot be removed during the time allotted, then an addendum extending the time limit must be initiated and signed by all parties to the original contract.

The obvious problem that can occur here is if the seller refuses to sign such an addendum. If he still wants to make the deal, then chances are that he will sign, if not signing would otherwise kill the deal. But suppose that in the meantime, a better offer has surfaced. The seller is certainly not going to extend any additional courtesies to the buyer when he has a better offer within grasp.

LOAN APPROVAL

As mentioned before, lending institutions look to two criteria in deciding whether or not to make a loan:

1) the credit-worthiness and ability to repay of the potential borrower;

2) the appraised value of the property.

Both are very important, but of the two, the property value is most important. Since the property usually represents the sole source of security in case of default, it is understandable that the banks place so much importance on the property value.

Actually, what they are really concerned with is the equity value above their loan. Banking decisions are made on loan-to-value ratios. The higher the ratio, the more concerned they are about the borrower's ability to repay.

If the loan-to-value ratio is greater than 80%, the lenders become quite concerned about the borrower's ability to repay and usually require private mortgage insurance to insure that portion of the mortgage over and above 80% in case of a default. As mentioned earlier, the cost of this insurance is borne by the borrower.

If the loan-to-value ratio is 75% or less, most lenders offer an easy qualifier whereby they don't even concern themselves with the borrower's ability to repay. The theory here is that the borrower has a significant amount of cash equity which he will not allow to be easily jeopardized, and even if he does get into trouble and cannot pay, the bank has sufficient equity in the property to insure against suffering any losses.

In any event, good credit is essential. No matter what the loan-to-value ratio, the first step in the loan process is to secure a credit report. With computerized nationwide credit reporting services such as TRW, this can be accomplished almost instantly. Many banks offer credit approval in twenty-four to forty-eight hours.

In addition to the credit report, the complete loan application package will require a formal application in all cases and employment and income verification forms to be completed except for easy qualifier loans.

Once all of this has been verified and approved, an appraisal will be ordered. Some lenders use in-house staff appraisers, while others hire independent fee appraisers. There is much discussion in the industry that the use of in-house staff appraisers is a conflict of interest, because staff employees can be unduly influenced to make appraisals come in higher than they should in order to make the loan.

Remember, lenders are in the business to make loans, and once the loan is made, most are sold on the secondary market.

If you are convinced that you bought the property for a fair price, then you simply want it to be appraised and have everything else go smoothly during the loan processing. Depending upon backlogs and availability of funds, the total approval process can take anywhere from as short as ten days to as long as sixty days. The norm is twenty to thirty days.

Once the loan has been approved, funding can usually take place within a few days, although it is possible that a loan might be approved to be funded out of the budget of the next period, which could delay the actual funding for several weeks.

Government insured or guaranteed loans involve a great deal more paperwork and red tape and usually take more time than conventional loans, however, because they often result in lower down payment requirements or slightly better interest rates, it is often worth the wait.

It should be carefully noted that once a loan is approved, the commitment is for a finite period of time. Most commitments are for thirty days, although it is possible to get a commitment for sixty days. In a highly volatile money market, you may not be able to receive a commitment for more than ten or fifteen days.

This can be a real problem when there are other contingencies which cannot be resolved within the time limit set in the mortgage commitment. The best example is when you are purchasing a house contingent upon the sale of your present house.

IT'S FINALLY YOURS: CLOSE OF ESCROW

The transfer of title is handled different ways in different parts of the country. When I was working real estate in Connecticut in the early 1970's, attor-

neys handled the escrows and also insured title.

In most parts of the country, title companies have taken over the process. In California, the process goes as follows:

An escrow is opened with the title company of choice by depositing the deposit into their trust account, which is often interest-bearing. At this point, the title company becomes the agent for both the seller and the buyer. The title company reviews the sales contract, makes certain all provisions are adhered to, orders payoffs for existing loans, requests loan documents for any new loans, sees to it that all documents are properly signed and notarized, searches the title, and insures title for the new owners.

Title companies play an essential and vital role in the sale and exchange of real property. It would be an act of pure foolishness to attempt to avoid the services of a title company.

Again referring to the procedure in California, the following is typical: All of the required documents are usually prepared several days before the actual close of escrow date, and the parties are invited to come in and sign at their convenience. Once all documents are signed and the loan documents are returned to the lender, the loan will then be funded. Finally, all required documents (deed, deed of trust, and note) are recorded and at that time the escrow is considered closed. This is normally a three-day process at best (signing, funding, and recording).

In our sample contract, possession was to take place at noon on the date escrow closed. Quite often, other arrangements are made out of necessity, but this is by far the cleanest and simplest, and lacks the potential for future problems.

There are several other items that should be mentioned briefly at this point.

Homeowner's insurance should be applied for and a notice of insurance must be in the hands of the escrow officer before the loan can be funded and the escrow closed.

Outside of escrow, the buyer should remember to contract for gas and electrical service as well as water, telephone, and garbage pickup. If these services are ordered sufficiently in advance of actual possession, then there is very little reason for any interruption in any of these services.

The only thing left now is to begin moving, which is not a whole lot of fun, but very soon that will be behind you and you can bask in the joy of owning your new home.

MOVING UP (OR DOWN, OR SIDEWAYS)

As I stated in the beginning, many people repeat this process many times during the course of their lives. Many start out quite modestly, but as the family grows and income increases, they parlay their way into bigger and better homes as the years go by. Others are forced to repeat the process due to relocation. We are a very mobile society. Finally, once the family has left, the empty nesters often find it desirable to move down into accommodations that are smaller and easier to live with — a new status in life.

Whatever the reason, the next move puts you in the role of buyer on the one hand and seller on the other. This is where the next section will come in handy.

Part 2
Selling a
Valued Possesion

6
Two Keys to a Successful Sale

Your home is a very personal possession. It is almost impossible not to experience some emotions when it finally comes time to sell, even if the purpose of the sale is to move on to something better.

Besides the financial burden of meeting those mortgage payments every month, a lot of sweat equity usually goes into the home. You have had fights and made love in that home. You may have made babies and raised those babies in that home. You may have lost a cherished loved one. Or experienced a bitter divorce. Whatever life has been like while you have lived there, the thought of selling cannot help but evoke certain emotions. Emotions come in many forms — joy, sorrow, anger, fear — but whatever they are, they are bound to cloud good business judgment if not kept in check.

Pride of ownership is a desirable part of home ownership, but it can be overwhelming when trying to make a reasonable valuation. If you are overly anxious to put bad memories behind, you may make a hasty decision that will turn out to be very expensive. Sentimental attachments to plants, trees, and fixtures that are now an integral part of the real estate have often been known to kill an otherwise excellent potential sale.

If you are human, then you are going to experience some emotion, if nothing more than just plain relief. Whatever your particular emotions happen to be, you must deal with them and get them under control before you tackle the business aspects of selling your home.

There is one sure way to do this. Think positive, and live for the future, not in the past. Emotions related to a home are also related to the past. Dwelling too deeply on the past can become morbid and downright disabling. My favorite saying is one we have all heard and one that I have used more than once to get myself in gear again and moving forward. That saying, "Today is the first day of the rest of my life," if said loud enough and truly recognized for its magnificent reality, can yank you out of the past and get you moving in a fresh new direction like nothing else on earth. Why? Because you are saying, "I believe in myself and to hell with the past because I have a great future ahead of me." Think about it. Then start thinking about the business of selling your home.

It takes just two basic elements to sell residential real estate: exposure and the right price. It sounds simple enough, and in theory, it is. It is fairly obvious that if nobody knows your house is for sale, it probably won't sell. So we have devoted a section to exploring all of the elements that go into achieving maximum exposure.

Furthermore, if a house is grossly overpriced, it will not sell. You will never even get an offer. Let me provide a theory as to why this is. As buyers look at lots of houses, they become pretty knowledgeable about market values, especially if they have read this book. When they see a house that they like, they will arrive at a figure that they might be willing to pay, based upon their own financial capabilities or what they think the property is worth. Now here is the rationale, which is best explained with an example.

Suppose the buyer finds a house which he feels is worth $250,000 and the asking price is $260,000. His natural inclination will be to offer $240,000 in order to arrive at a halfway point of $250,000, the price he is willing to pay. Now in this example, he will probably make the offer and a deal might well be struck if, indeed, the property is truly worth $250,000.

Suppose, however, that the buyer thinks the house is worth $250,000, but the asking price is $300,000. In order to evoke the same barter theory, the buyer would have to make an offer of $200,000 in order to arrive at a mid-point of $250,000. There are very few buyers brash enough to make a $200,000 offer on a property with an asking price of $300,000. Instead, they simply walk away.

Next argument. If the real estate agent has properly qualified the buyer, the agent will know the maximum price the buyer can afford. The agent might show homes a little above the maximum, figuring that there may be a little room to negotiate. There is no way the agent is going to show homes priced significantly beyond the buyer's ability and have the buyer fall in love with something too expensive. And remember, the multiple listing books present the listings in order of price, so as an agent scans the book for listings to show the potential buyer, he will never see or consider your property, even though its fair market value might be within the buyer's price range, if your property is grossly overpriced.

Overpriced listings do not sell. I took a listing about a year ago for $298,000, which turned out to be way overpriced. The property was shown continuously, but no offers were forthcoming. After six months and a succession of price reductions, we finally arrived at a price of $249,500. That price seemed to break the barrier. We sold the property within a week for $238,000 and had two backup offers. We wasted a lot of time and effort and caused the owner some inconvenience and concern because we did not price the property properly in the first place.

So remember, the two keys to a timely and successful sale are EXPOSURE and PRICE.

DETERMINING MARKET VALUE

There are three basic methods utilized by appraisers to determine real estate values. They are called the cost approach, the income approach, and the market approach.

The income approach is strictly used for income-producing properties, which is not the subject at hand.

The cost approach can occasionally be helpful in evaluating single family homes, especially if they are unusual and there are no comparable homes available to perform a valid market comparison. In using the cost approach, the appraiser actually breaks the property down into its various building components and estimates the material, labor, and overhead that would be required to duplicate the existing structure. He would then depreciate this figure based upon the age and condition of the structure and add the depreciated figure to the estimated land value to arrive at a value utilizing the cost approach.

The market approach, however, is the most utilized method of evaluating owner-occupied residential real estate. This is the method used by real estate agents trying to determine market value prior to listing, and bank appraisers trying to determine loan value.

Comparables

In the market approach, the appraiser or real estate agent will search for properties similar to the subject properties that have sold in the recent past. They will then attempt to economically adjust the sale price of each comparable for time (inflation), location, lot size, number of rooms, condition, and anything else that will adjust the value of the comparable to more nearly reflect the value of the subject property.

If your house is in a subdivision of two hundred homes, and there are only two or three models in the whole subdivision, then it is a very simple matter to pull up recent sales from that subdivision and determine a very precise market value for your particular model. If your home is custom-built with many unique features on some acreage that also has some unique characteristics, then determining the value of your property could be quite a challenge.

It must be remembered that this method of determining value is not an exact science, and the greater the dissimilarities between the comparables and the subject property, the greater the margin for error.

Remember also that the vast majority of residential real estate agents are not qualified appraisers. That is why the smart agent will refer to his work as a "Market Evaluation" or a "Comparative Market Analysis" instead of an appraisal. An opinion of value should not be labeled as an appraisal unless it has been prepared by a person certified as an appraiser by one of the leading appraiser associations.

This is not to say, however, that these opinions of values based upon recent comparable sales and provided by real estate agents are not valuable, because they are. It does mean that some are a great deal more valuable than others.

The reasons for this are many and varied. First, there is a subjectiveness to this whole process that should be understood. It starts with the agent's choice of comparables. It would not be unusual for two different agents to use two entirely different sets of comparables as each worked up an opinion of value for the same property. As you might imagine, it would stand to reason that each would come up with a different value based simply on the fact that they chose different comparables.

To carry the subjectiveness a little further, suppose one agent thought the house was just great while the other agent did not care for it at all. This personal opinion might have a great deal to do with the comparables that each chose. Even if they used the same comparables, each agent is going to view the property relative to these comparables based upon that personal opinion. About now you might say, "Wait a minute. Isn't the agent supposed to be a professional here? How can he let personal opinion get involved?" The really professional agents will try very hard not to let their personal feelings interfere with their judgment, but agents are human too. And remember, if personal feelings do get in the way, they can result in opinions of value that are unreasonably high just as often as those that are valued too low.

As I mentioned earlier, the more unusual the property, the more difficult it is to come up with a really good comparative market analysis. Here is where experience really pays off. The very experienced, very active agent knows the comparables much better than the newcomer. Furthermore, the experienced agent is usually better equipped to make the more complex adjustments in value from comparable to subject property than the newer agent. Finally, an experienced agent develops an intimacy with the marketplace that often results in a "gut feeling" that frequently turns out to be far more accurate than all the appraisals that could ever be done.

Unscrupulous Practices

Now I must get into a discussion I do not enjoy. It has to do with what I consider unscrupulous practices utilized by more than just a few agents in the business of obtaining listings. It is one thing for an agent to come up with an erroneous value out of ignorance or because emotion got in the way. It is an entirely different matter when an agent knowingly either overstates or understates an opinion of value.

The less common but more serious of the two is when the agent purposely understates the value. He would only do this for one of two reasons. First, he realizes that at the particular price, he can make a quick sale with virtually no effort or expense on his part. Even worse, he has in mind some way to make a personal gain by pricing the property below market. Either way, he is cheating his clients, the sellers, out of funds that are rightfully theirs. Many of these unscrupulous agents have been weeded out of the real estate industry, but some remain and caution should be observed.

The other practice which I consider unscrupulous is the practice of knowingly overstating the value. This is often referred to as "buying the listing." In this scenario, the agent will tell the client exactly what the client wants to hear — that his home is worth a lot more than it really is. This agent is banking on the assumption that other competing agents will come in at more realistic values and that the seller will list with him thinking that he will realize a greater profit by doing so. What really happens is that nothing happens. After a few weeks or a month, the agent starts pressuring the seller to reduce the price, which was part of the plan from the beginning. The result of such tactics is not only a great deal of wasted time and aggravation in getting the property sold, but often a price below what it would have garnered if it had been priced right in the first place. This happens simply because a home on the market too long is presumed to have something wrong with it that is not immediately obvious.

Remember this: figures don't lie, but liars sure can figure. By the time you have finished this book, you should be able to recognize a professional and honest agent when you see one, and you will be equipped to make valid real estate decisions on your own, independent of the agent.

Make Your Own Comparisons

Now it's time to give you some tools that will at least let you double check the validity of your agent's opinion of value. However, before we do this, let's realize that your agent is in a far better position to come up with the comparable information than you are. So this discussion assumes that you have an agent who at least is providing the source of information.

First off, you should get in your car and go out and personally look at each comparable that the agent has chosen. If you have an instant camera handy, it would help to take a picture. If you can get inside any of these houses, all the better. But for the most part, this will not be possible. You can tell a lot from the outside, and you should make notes.

Now it is time to compare these properties with yours. If you think agents get subjective about houses, let me tell you about sellers. Sellers are rarely capable of being totally objective about their home and its value. If you are different — great. But remember, I warned you. So try very hard to be as objective as possible. If the other house has better landscaping — say so. Remember, cheating here is like cheating at solitaire. There is only one player.

In making these value comparisons, different criteria have different rankings in importance. Location tops the list. Property values will vary greatly from one community to another. It may have just evolved this way, but more often it has happened by design. Good planning and zoning and individual involvement in community affairs are often major factors in future real estate values in that community. Specific neighborhoods within a town can also make a major difference. A quiet street vs. a busy street will affect value. The proximity of freeways, railroads, and airports will affect value. If they are so close that you can hear them, the value will be decreased. If they are so far away it makes commuting difficult, that might also result in a decrease in value. They should be convenient but not too close.

After location comes size, architectural style, and condition. It's difficult to say which is more important, but I think size probably wins out by a nose.

Size means several things. A half-acre lot is certainly more desirable than a quarter-acre lot. A 2,200 square foot house is more desirable than an 1,800 square foot. But which is more desirable, a 2,200 square foot house on a quarter-acre or an 1,800 square foot house on a half-acre? This is where judgment and knowledge of the local area becomes very important. Size may be the same, but the room configuration is different. Three bedrooms are more desirable than two. Two baths are more desirable than one. And so on.

Next, I think, comes condition. Most buyers cannot see beyond what is staring them in the face. We will talk more about this a little later, but suffice it to say that houses in disrepair or littered with junk autos and a multitude of other items most people find distasteful are worth a lot less than homes that are neat and clean and in good repair with well-maintained lawns.

There is a wide variety of architectural styles in housing, and there seems to be someone for just about every style, no matter how exotic. But on average, traditional never seems to go out of favor. What is traditional in one part of the country may

not be in another. A Cape Cod colonial is very traditional in New England but quite scarce in Arizona. In most parts of the country, ultra-contemporary has never really caught on with the general public. Many years ago, I had a builder friend in Atlanta who built magnificent contemporary homes. He told me one day that he realized that his homes appealed to less than ten percent of the population, but since he was the only builder specializing in this style at the time, he hoped to have the contemporary buffs all to himself. He was very successful. However, everything else being equal, a contemporary will probably not have as big a market as a traditional, and therefore may not command as high a price. The reverse of this could be true if you can find that rare individual buyer who just can't live without a contemporary house, but the odds are against it.

After weighing all of the factors without getting too scientific about the whole thing, you will begin to appreciate how the process works. At the very least, you should be able to detect an incompetent job on the part of the agent. At best, you should be able to provide a very professional critique of the agent's work.

Getting the Facts

You might be thinking that at very best you could do the job without the agent at all. That might well be true IF you have the means to gather the true facts. Over the years, I have been absolutely amazed when prospective clients have informed me with great certainty about the price and conditions of the sale of neighboring homes. The reason for my amazement is because I know from public record or personal knowledge that their absolute indisputable facts are totally erroneous. Most people are very private about their personal finances. And the ones who do talk usually exaggerate. This is important stuff. Don't attempt to place a value on your home based on anything short of cold hard facts.

There are a variety of forms and formats in use to accumulate and convey this information. Appendix S-1 is an example of a Comparative Market Analysis (CMA) as used by Fellowes Realty.

As can be seen from the example, some real time and effort are required to do a first-class job. Very often the buyer is in a great rush and puts incredible pressure on the agent to get him a price — NOW! Panicked by the pressure and the fear of losing a listing opportunity, the agent may take shortcuts in preparing his opinion of value. Agents are often besieged with requests to provide these analyses to people who are looking to refinance or are just plain curious. Most agents are very happy to provide this service free of charge in the hopes that it will pay dividends sometime in the future. But anyone requesting such information should realize that it is going to take some time. How much time? Depending upon the agent's work load, it should be completed in 48-72 hours. If it takes less time, then either the agent has absolutely nothing else to do or he has not done all of his homework. If it is going to take longer than seventy-two hours, then the agent should inform the client.

Once market value has been ascertained and agreed upon, then it is time to determine a pricing strategy. A property should never be priced more than 10% above market if you are really serious about selling, and generally speaking, 10% is too high. Here is a good rule of thumb. If the house is easily compared because there are lots of houses just like it that have sold recently, then keep the price close to market, not more than 2-3%. If the property is unusual, then add in a bit more cushion to cover any possible errors in the evaluation. In this case, 5-7% might be appropriate depending upon its unique features.

ACHIEVING MAXIMUM EXPOSURE

A house won't sell if nobody knows it is for sale. That seems fairly obvious. In this section we will talk about all of the tools that can be utilized to market residential real estate. The Marketing Plan (Appendix S-2) provides an outline of one realty company's marketing strategy.

Multiple Listing Service

Your local Board of Realtors controls the single most effective tool that has ever been utilized in marketing residential real estate — the local Multiple Listing Service. Since this service has been computerized, it has become absolutely indispensable to the residential real estate industry. Usually within hours after your property is listed, it is entered into the computer, making it immediately available to every agent who is a member of the service. Often, this means that literally hundreds of agents have been drawn into the process of marketing your home.

In most areas, the service provides the listing information in two forms. First, it resides in memory in the computer, and is available for the asking. For those of you familiar with computers, this service is a large data base that can be sorted in many ways. For instance, if you ask for all properties in a particular area with three bedrooms and two baths and priced between $100,000 and $125,000, the computer will provide the current listings that meet all of the criteria.

In addition to providing information on currently listed properties, the computer also stores information on recently sold properties. This information is usually retained in memory for one to two years. This is where your agent will start in his search for comparables.

Without getting too far off of the subject, it should be mentioned that the computerization of the MLS has also made possible at no extra cost a great deal of statistical data such as average sales prices, numbers of sales per period, and much more.

The other way in which the MLS presents the data

is by publishing it in book form. New books are usually distributed either every week or every other week. The advantage to the book is that there are usually pictures and all of the information is available simply by turning pages. Furthermore, the book can be easily carried around with the agent as he travels through his territory, whereas the computer cannot. The major disadvantage of the book is that its information is not always currently correct, since changes are constantly occurring between publication dates.

Many agents will take a listing, enter it into the MLS, throw up a sign, and then sit back and wait for something to happen. No good. Even as powerful a tool as the MLS has become, the listing agent still has many additional tools available to him to market your property effectively.

First of all, it is not enough simply to make other agents aware of the property, it is important that they actually see it. Out of sight, out of mind. Get enough agents through the property, and more than likely one or more of them will think of someone who would like to see the property. There are two basic schemes utilized to get agents to view properties.

Company Tour

Most of the larger companies have weekly sales meetings, and at the end of each meeting they will usually have a tour of their new listings. This is sort of a sneak preview before the property is fully exposed to the industry at large.

Board of Realtors Tour

The second, and more important from a pure exposure point of view, is the weekly Board of Realtors tour. The realtors and their agents (realtor associates) usually have a short meeting first thing in the morning and then go off to tour new listings. Since there are often more listings than there is time to get to them all, agents have to pick and

choose which listing to visit. A smart listing agent will often offer refreshments as an enticement to get as many agents as possible to visit his tour property. In most boards, it is quite proper to tour your property once a month, but not more often than that.

Flyers and Brochures

Just as quickly as possible, a flyer or brochure should be prepared highlighting the features and pertinent information regarding the property. These should be left in the home, mailed to other agents, and given to each prospective buyer. The amount of money that can economically be spent on these will be determined by the value of the property, but even the simplest flyer should be created neatly and attractively on a good quality paper. If the agent is properly equipped, he will neatly type up a master which can be used to reproduce the data on pre-printed background forms specifically designed for flyers by running them through the photocopy machine.

If a more elaborate brochure with pictures is in order, it will take some time to have this laid out and reproduced. The flyers should be utilized in the interim.

It is important that a prospective buyer or a prospective buyer's agent have some descriptive material in hand after seeing the property. Again, out of sight, out of mind. Often, buyers will see so many houses in one day that they cannot distinguish one from the other.

For Sale Sign

Believe it or not, with all of the other tools utilized in selling homes, the For Sale sign in the front yard still accounts for a large portion of the sales that transpire. Real estate agencies have known for a long time that For Sale signs are the number one reason for making their phones ring.

Many sellers think putting up a For Sale sign is too personal. They want everyone in the world to know that their house is for sale except their neighbors. Impossible. If your home is marketed properly, then there will be so much activity going on that the neighbors will know the score in no time flat. So don't object to a For Sale sign. It's a powerful marketing tool.

MLS Lock Box

Most MLS's provide their members with keys which open lock boxes. The lock boxes are secured behind the doorknob or some other place, such as around a waste pipe or to an iron gate, where they cannot be removed. Inside the box is a key to the house. This system allows an agent to show the property without either the owner or the listing agent being present. History has proven that it is very rare that the security of the sellers has been compromised by the widespread use of this system.

Furthermore, it has also been well documented that if you make it too difficult for an agent to show a property, he just won't bother. The most accepted procedure is to set up instructions in the listing to have the agent call first for an appointment. If he gets no answer, then he can proceed and use the lock box.

Even if the agent has made an appointment, it is wise for the owners to vacate at the appointed time so the prospective buyers can view the property without the sellers hanging around. If the sellers are at home, the buyer may feel uncomfortable and hurry through the inspection. Also, the buyers are understandably reticent about expressing their feelings about the property in front of the sellers, especially if some of those feelings are negative. If the agent cannot get these feelings out on the table, then he has no way of dealing with them. Finally, it is easier for a buyer to picture himself living in a house if he is not seeing someone else living in it.

Public Open Houses

Sunday open houses do work. They work especially well for the agent. Even if someone walking through doesn't want that particular house, the agent often has the opportunity to suggest another.

More important to you, the seller, is the fact that open houses do often contribute to the sale of the property. Sometimes the ultimate buyer is first exposed to the property through the open house. Occasionally, an offer is made right on the spot. Agents showing properties on Sundays find it very convenient to take their clients to houses being held open. This helps alleviate the tight scheduling because no appointment is necessary. And finally, many buyers who are still undecided will often come back on their own during an open house so that they can have a second or third look before making up their minds.

Advertising

Newspaper and *Homes* magazine advertising represents a major part of most real estate agency budgets. There is usually a running conflict between the agents screaming for more advertising and the broker trying to keep his business in the black.

These ads do make the phone ring, and occasionally someone does buy the home that he called about, but this is not the case very often. When a potential buyer calls relative to a For Sale sign, at least he has seen the property from the outside and likes what he saw enough to make the phone call.

Newspaper advertising can be considerably more deceptive and is indeed designed to whet the appetite and make the phone ring. It sets an image for the agency. The bigger the ad, the bigger (and more successful) the agency is perceived to be, although this may not be true.

The newspaper is the best media to announce and

direct people to open houses. This is probably the most productive activity for newspaper advertising.

Finally, a certain amount of newspaper advertising is placed just to placate the sellers. Many sellers will simply raise hell if their house is not advertised each and every week, which is totally unreasonable. But most brokers end up caving in to some extent just to keep harmony.

In addition to local newspaper advertising, there is a selection of national and even international publications designed to promote very expensive properties. The costs to advertise in these publications are very high, usually involving both a flat fee and a percentage of the sale price. In most cases this is simply not justified, but on occasion it might be.

Direct Mail

There are several ways to utilize mailings effectively to sell listings. A first and easy mailing would be to the neighbors. This should include a flyer or brochure with a cover letter inviting them to an open house and suggesting that they might have friends who might be interested in becoming neighbors.

Some agents, including me, maintain a mailing list of the top producing agents in the communities that they serve. We will mail a brochure or flyer with a nice cover letter to each of these agents announcing each new listing that we receive.

If your property is located in a popular vacation or second home area, such as the Monterey peninsula, it would be smart to mail to the leading brokers there. For example, mailings to the San Francisco Bay area and the central valley of California would be a good idea.

Personal Rapport

Finally, the agent with a large number of personal contacts, both business and social, will have the best opportunity to provide exposure for your property through nothing more than word of mouth. The referral systems that some agents have built up over the years are quite awesome.

As you can see, there is a great deal that your agent can and should do to expose fully your property to the home buyers' marketplace. As a seller, you deserve it all and have every right to expect it. This discussion should also help you to appreciate that a good agent can utilize many more tools to market a property than an owner trying to go it alone. This is just one more reason why a truly professional agent is worth every dime he earns.

7
Setting the Stage

We have talked about the two basic keys to a successful sale — price and exposure. Now we need to discuss how to prepare the property to maximize the value and get it sold in the shortest possible time.

Although it would seem quite logical to make whatever changes are necessary to maximize the value, this is an area that sometimes requires financial decisions and can often evoke some strong emotions.

Stand back and view the property as a prospective buyer might view it. This is not easy, and is another area where the professional agent can help mightily. The more objective you can be, the more you will realize that the way you live in a home is definitely not the same as the way you sell a home. In order to be totally successful in selling your home, you are temporarily going to have to change your lifestyle. Appendix S-3: Preparing Your Home for Sale, as well as the text below looks at some of the things that really are necessary on your part to make this a successful sale.

CHANGING YOUR LIFESTYLE

First of all, any time the house is being shown, you should make yourself scarce. This is especially true during open houses. Now this is definitely an inconvenience, but it is extremely important. Prospective buyers simply will not open up in front of the seller. If you don't know the objections, you cannot overcome them.

Next, many of your household items which are an inherent part of your lifestyle or memorabilia of the past, will very often inhibit maximizing value. The reason is really very simple. The important thing is to allow the buyer to picture himself living in the house. If the house literally reeks of your lifestyle and your past, it may be impossible to picture anyone else in this environment.

Here is what a good agent is going to suggest. If you have collections and knickknacks on display, especially if they are valuable, put them away. If you are a hunter or fisherman and have trophies hanging on the walls, put them away. This is a major turn-off for many people who are into animal rights.

Clean up kitchen and bathroom counters, leaving only the bare essentials out. Remove notes and kids' drawings, etc. from the refrigerator door. If there are lots of hanging plants, some may have to be rearranged or even removed if they inhibit a clear view or tend to make rooms appear smaller. This is also true of furniture. Too many large pieces of furniture in a room tend to overwhelm and make the room appear much smaller than it really is. Some furniture might have to be stored in the garage. Finally, things that are somewhat inappropriate for a particular room should not be there. For instance, a bedroom should look like a bedroom and a family room should look like a family room. If a piece of exercise equipment or a computer or some hobby-in-process is set up in either one, it detracts. Pack it up for the time being. You are going to be moving soon anyway.

The things that we have discussed thus far will cost nothing but a little time and inconvenience. Mostly, it means that you will have to start packing a little sooner than you had anticipated. From here on, we will be talking about things that cost real money, and discussing the pros and cons of spending that money.

REPAIRS AND COSMETIC SURGERY

The first group of items require very minor expenditures and is highly recommended. It includes the repair of leaky faucets and loose door knobs and any other items that can easily be fixed or replaced with just a little time and effort. This certainly includes spackling holes in walls and replacing broken glass.

The next items are cosmetic and may cost a little bit more, but are very important. Have the carpets professionally cleaned. Not only will they look better, but it will also help to remove any pet odors. Wherever necessary, repaint. This is highly recommended on the inside of the house.

The outside represents a greater economic consideration. Clean up the landscaping. Curb appeal is very important. You know what they say about first impressions. How much money to spend on the outside of the house becomes an individual problem that cannot be given a blanket solution.

Needless to say, the expenditure must be less than the value enhancement that it provides.

As I said in the beginning of this book, selling a house is not a fun experience. You are seriously inconvenienced and your lifestyle is compromised. However, knowing this up front makes living with it a lot easier. Why? By recognizing ahead of time what is involved, you will be a lot more inclined to do all of the right things the first time around. These are all of the things we have talked about thus far: associate with the right agent, price the property right, stage the property to show at its very best, and insist on all of the marketing tools available to guarantee maximum exposure. Finally, if you expect the worst, you will probably be pleasantly surprised that it was not nearly as bad as you had anticipated.

YOUR LEGAL RIGHTS AND RESPONSIBILITIES

This section may seem familiar because it is somewhat redundant to the same heading in the section for buyers. As stated in that section, there is no intent in this book to provide legal advice, and you should always consult an attorney when such advice is required. Furthermore, the laws vary from state to state and it would be impossible to provide accurate advice even if there was such an intent.

Again, this is also the proper time to point out that in the sections to follow, numerous legal documents will be utilized as examples. The documents chosen are those used by the Menlo-Atherton Board of Realtors in California, because they are the most complete that I know of, and they are also the ones with which I am most familiar. The documents that you will be confronted with will most likely be different in both form and content. After these discussions you may find that the forms being utilized in your area seem grossly inadequate. If this is the case and you are truly concerned, you can either ask that certain paragraphs be added, or you can hire an attorney to prepare the forms for you. You do not have to sign forms that you are not comfortable with.

Whether these documents are prepared by an attorney or a real estate agent or anyone else, they are legally binding documents that are an integral part of selling a home. The way these documents are structured will be extremely important in both protecting your legal rights and limiting your liabilities.

Many legal complications can arise in the course of selling a home. The legal documents used in completing these transactions are constantly being refined and improved to reflect the changing needs of our increasingly complex society. The local Boards of Realtors, with great assistance from both the state and national associations of realtors, labor endlessly in an effort to produce forms that will eliminate ambiguity and clearly define each party's rights and responsibilities in the transaction.

The forms, however, are only a guideline for avoiding future problems. They are really of very little value if they are sloppily or incompletely prepared. This is where a really professional agent earns his keep. As we shall see shortly, the way these forms are prepared can either properly define the terms of the transaction and protect the rights of the parties concerned or result in devastation for one or both of the parties.

The real purpose of all of these documents is to spell out the true intent of all of the parties to the transaction. If the true intent of any of the parties is devious or in any way different than that proclaimed, then problems are likely to arise no matter how great a set of documents everyone thinks they have.

Intent and motivation: these are the keys to a successful transaction. If you have a motivated seller who fully intends to sell and a motivated buyer who fully intends to fulfill his end of the bargain, then somehow the transaction will close and every-

one will part at least reasonably satisfied. However, if one of the parties is playing games and not being straight, then the whole transaction is flirting with disaster. Again, the various documents are designed to help avoid the problems that can arise from such a situation, but an experienced and knowledgeable agent can usually sense and find ways to combat these situations before they get out of hand.

Again, let me emphasize: if you do not feel completely comfortable with what you are being asked to sign, see an attorney first.

WHAT YOU SHOULD EXPECT FROM YOUR AGENT

Let's start by discussing the selection of an agent to market your home. Being a friend, relative, or neighbor is simply not reason enough to hire an agent. Now if that friend, relative, or neighbor is also an extremely competent real estate agent whom you like and trust, then by all means, hire that agent.

You will note that I use the word "hire" because that is exactly what you will be doing. You will hire an agent to market your home and you will pay that agent a fair compensation for doing so out of the proceeds of the sale. That agent may in turn split this fee with some other agent for bringing a buyer to you, but the listing agent is the one you are hiring; he or she will be your direct link to everything that goes on relative to the entire process of the marketing and closing of escrow on your home.

Anyone that you hire, you can also fire. Do not let anyone lead you to believe that because you have signed an exclusive listing agreement for some definite time period, and you discover that you made a poor choice of agents, that you cannot cancel that agreement. You can. If your agent is simply not performing as promised, you have every right to cancel the listing agreement. This should be done in writing and you should not consider it cancelled until you receive written confirmation from the broker to that effect. If the broker is not cooperative in this respect, then you can write directly to the real estate commissioner in your state. The mere threat of such action will normally get the broker's attention and cooperation.

Now this certainly does not mean that you have no responsibility as a result of signing a listing agreement. You do. For one thing, if a purchase agreement was signed prior to cancelling the listing agreement, then you would still be liable for a commission to the agent. This is fairly cut and dried. But if a prospective buyer was shown your property prior to your cancellation of the listing agreement, and then a purchase agreement was entered into subsequent to that cancellation, a question would arise as to whom, if anyone, you owed a commission. There have been numerous cases over the years where a seller has cancelled out one agent and agreed to pay a commission to another agent, only to find that he is legally obligated to also pay the first agent. Great care should be exercised in making sure that your obligation to one agent is completely ended before entering into another contract with a second agent.

Finally, if an agent has not fulfilled your expectations, no matter how unrealistic, can you or should you cancel your listing agreement? I would venture to say that in most states, if you want to cancel, you can cancel, no matter what the reason. Morally, whether you should or not, is another matter. If that agent has reinforced those unrealistic expectations, then that agent deserves to be cancelled.

On the other hand, if the agent was truthful with you from the very beginning, but you chose not to take his advice and now you are finding that nothing is happening, who can you blame? If I were you, I would get serious and lower my expectations. Barring this, if I were the agent, I would cancel the listing. People who are hired can also quit.

FINDING AN AGENT

Obviously, the best solution is to find the right agent in the first place and avoid all of the hassle. If you know someone who has sold in your neighborhood, you may want to inquire about who the agent was and how satisfied he was with that person's performance. You can also seek recommendations from local banks, attorneys, and title companies.

You may have received periodic mailings from one or more agents. This is probably the result of what is known in the industry as "farming." An agent will pick a relatively small geographical area and concentrate very hard on that area. He will try to learn everything there is to know about the area, including market values and trends. Agents who farm are usually fairly dedicated hardworking people. Someone who has been mailing into your area for some time might not be a bad choice to hire as your listing agent.

The practice of inviting several agents to make a listing presentation is highly recommended. If an agent is not willing to perform in a competitive environment, then he has no place in the real estate business. This gives you an opportunity to hear the presentations and promises of agents from several different real estate companies. DO NOT INVITE TWO AGENTS FROM ONE COMPANY. This is sure to cause internal strife which will be counter-productive in marketing your property. One recommendation: choose agents from companies that seem to be fairly active in your marketplace on an on-going basis.

Ask how he plans to market your property, not just generalities, but specifics. Will he produce a flyer or brochure, and what will it look like? How often will open houses be held? What will be the advertising plan? How will the property be exposed to other agents?

Next, you want to feel certain that he knows what he is talking about relative to the value he places on your property. How detailed is his analysis? Has he used fair comparisons? Does he appear confident and comfortable in making this presentation? Are you confident and comfortable that he knows what he is talking about? As we have already discussed, getting the price right to begin with is of crucial importance.

Next, is this agent going to help you in the staging of your property? You may never have heard of such a thing before reading it here, but believe me, it is very important in maximizing the value and minimizing the time on the market. If the agent does not mention this on his own, he probably has no intention of providing this aspect of the service, or he is afraid of bringing it up for fear of offending you. The strong agent will find a diplomatic way of broaching this sometimes delicate subject.

Finally, you simply need to feel comfortable with your agent. You have to feel certain that he is honest and has your best interests at heart. Even if everything else seems great, but his voice grates on your nerves or he demonstrates a trait or habit you find annoying, forget it. It is not going to work. The task that you are about to undertake has aspects that can be unpleasant. The relationship needs to be pleasant. Comfortable, pleasant, and professional. That is what we should be striving for here.

THE LISTING AGREEMENT

In this section we will go through a standard Multiple Listing Service agreement. Please refer to Appendix S-4 as I explain the agreement. Appendix S-5 is the MLS Fact Sheet (also known as a Profile Sheet) used for recording all pertinent information about the property for sale.

Referring now to the MLS agreement, please note that it starts out stating that it is for the exclusive use of MLS members and that it is intended to be a legally binding document. We have discussed the legal ramifications earlier, but they will continue to come up as we work our way through the agreement.

Paragraph 1 names the Broker (not the individual sales agent) being employed, a description of the property being listed, the list price, and the terms. Please note that the broker is hereinafter referred to as Agent and that this is an Exclusive Right to Sell. This means that for the duration of this listing agreement, no one (including the owner) can sell this property without paying the Agent a commission. This is generally the only form of listing acceptable in the various MLS's in existence in the U.S.

There are two other types of listings. The first is an Exclusive Agency, which means that the employed Agent is the only one other than the owner who can sell the property without a commission being due to the Agent. Finally, an Open Listing means that anyone with a listing can sell the property as well as the owner, and whoever sells it (except the owner) gets the commission. Very few agents are willing to expend much time or effort in marketing a property without an exclusive listing. No matter what the listing form, it should be in writing to be enforceable.

Paragraph 2 sets the beginning and expiration dates of the agreement. It is important to note that a commission is deemed earned if a ready, willing, and able buyer is procured to purchase the property at precisely the price and terms specified in paragraph 1, even if the seller decides not to sell at the last minute.

Paragraph 3 concerns the amount of the brokerage fee. BROKERAGE FEES ARE NOT FIXED BY LAW AND ARE NEGOTIABLE. The customary fee for years has been and still is 6%. Fees both higher and lower than 6% can be negotiated, however, it will generally be borne out that you will get pretty much what you pay for.

If a lower fee is negotiated, say 5%, then very often the cooperating agents will avoid showing the property if they are asked to share in the reduction by receiving 2.5% (half of 5%) instead of the normal 3% (half of 6%). If the listing agent takes on the whole reduction himself by offering 3% to the cooperating Agents and keeping only 2%, then he will not be able to afford to devote as much time, effort, and money to marketing the property as he might have otherwise. Many an agent is perfectly happy to cut a commission because they never intended to spend much time, effort, or money to begin with.

This is not to say that commissions should never be negotiated. It is to say that this is not the right time to do it. It is far better to list the property at the going rate for a price that you would not mind paying with the full commission. Then, if things get really tough during the negotiating of a purchase agreement, that may be the time to expect a little help from the agents involved in order to make the transaction come together.

Remember this: most agents feel that their commissions are hard-earned and are very reluctant to cut them, and they have every right to be adequately paid for their services just as a doctor or lawyer or anyone else. Real estate agencies have huge overheads and all across the country they have found 6% to be marginal in order to make a profit. So don't be surprised if you run into serious resistance when you attempt to cut into your agent's livelihood.

Paragraph 4 deals with the disposition of the deposit in the case of a buyer default. It simply states that seller and agent agree to split fifty-fifty whatever deposit is available at the time of default, except that the agent's share cannot exceed the commission to which he would normally be entitled. In reality, this is simply an agreement between seller and agent in the event that the deposit can be retained as liquidated damages in case of default. The ability to retain these funds has a great deal to do with how the purchase contract is written. This

is discussed in greater detail in the appropriate sections.

Paragraph 5 is the interesting result of buyers who allow an agent to spend a great deal of time and effort in showing them properties and then attempt to go around the agent and deal directly with the seller, in the hopes of cutting a better deal. You will note that the seller is obligated to pay a commission to the listing agent for a specified period of time after the agreement has expired if the property is sold to a prospective buyer who was shown the property during the term of the agreement. The exception to this is when the property is re-listed with another agent. The theory, of course, is that the seller will have to pay a commission in any event, so there is little incentive to play games with the original listing agent.

Paragraph 6 states that the property will be maintained in at least its present state and condition for the duration of the agreement or until close of escrow, and that the seller will allow the property to be shown during reasonable hours. It also states that the appliances and basic systems are in working order, except as noted.

Paragraph 7 delineates who will pay for the title insurance and escrow charges. It also spells out the method of proration of insurance, taxes, rent, homeowner's association dues, etc. These terms may be altered in the offer to purchase, but the seller is obligated to the terms as spelled out in this agreement unless he agrees otherwise.

Paragraph 8 spells out how county and/or city transfer taxes are to be paid.

Paragraph 9 deals with disclosures. These are all applicable in California but may or may not be applicable in other states. I will discuss each one individually.

a) Offer of sub-agency: This has to do with the age-old question of dual agency. As has been mentioned elsewhere, there is a conflict between acceptable real estate practice and the letter of the law, especially in California. The law states that an agent's fiduciary responsibility is to whomever pays the commission. This is almost always the seller. In most areas, the agent procuring a buyer is considered a sub-agent of the listing agent, hence also an agent of the seller. It is quite clear that if this agent is representing the buyer and the seller at the same time, a conflict exists.

In Santa Clara and San Mateo counties of California, a number of Boards of Realtors have adopted a policy whereas the listing agent specifically states that no offer of sub-agency is intended. This does not mean that he will not split a commission with other agents. It does mean that both he and the seller refuse to consider other agents as being employed by the seller and further relieves both the other agents. This is very progressive thinking and should be seriously considered by realtors everywhere. It does not, in my opinion, eliminate the conflict between practice and the letter of the law.

b) This simply states whether or not there will be a For Sale sign. As mentioned previously, For Sale signs are strong marketing tools.

c) Will a lock box be placed on the property? Lock boxes provide tremendous accessibility to the brokerage community and usually result in a greater number of showings.

d) We cover home protection plans when we discuss the purchase agreement, however, the seller should be advised that such plans exist, so that he will have the opportunity to decide whether or not to purchase one to facilitate the marketing of his property.

e) These special study zones have to do with proximity to earthquake epicenters and fault lines. This one is peculiar to California.

f) Zones have also been set up for areas susceptible to flooding due to unusually high tides.

g) Items 9(e) and 9(f) are simply a statement of the seller's and/or his agent's opinion as to whether the property falls into one of these zones. This item determines whether or not the seller intends to provide a report from a competent authority concerning one or both of these zones.

h) A structural pest control report is going to be required (at least in California) sooner or later. This item simply determines whether or not the seller will provide this information up front. I highly recommend that it be done.

i) If there are Covenants, Conditions, and Restrictions (CC&R's) to which the property is subject, they should be furnished by the seller to a potential buyer. Any other community data would be helpful, but is not mandatory.

j) This law was enacted to prevent foreign sellers skipping off to their native lands without paying their capital gains tax to Uncle Sam. (See Appendix S-6.) Under this act, the BUYER is required by law to deduct on behalf of the IRS 10% of the sales price unless: 1) he is provided by the seller an affidavit stating that seller is not a "foreign person"; 2) he is provided with an IRS "qualifying statement" by the seller; or 3) the purchase price is $300,000 or less and the buyer intends to live in the property at least 50% of the time over the next two years. If this is not adhered to, the buyer could be potentially liable for this tax if the IRS is unsuccessful in collecting from the seller.

Paragraph 10 requires the seller to list any work that has been done (to his knowledge) without building permits. This is a part of the full disclosure that has become so important (at least in California) in recent years.

Paragraph 11 is a hold harmless clause releasing the agent from liability resulting from incorrect or incomplete information supplied by the seller. It also excuses the agent from responsibility for vandalism, theft, or damage to the property.

Paragraph 12 is a standard clause concerning attorney's fees in the case of a dispute.

Paragraph 13 is the non-discrimination statement.

Paragraph 14 refers to dual agency, which is covered in detail under the discussion of the purchase contract.

Finally, the Listing Agreement must be dated and signed by all parties concerned, including the listing broker, who would normally not be present at the time the agreement is executed. Therefore, it will be necessary for the agent to secure his broker's signature and return a copy to the seller.

Along with the Listing Agreement, it is also necessary for the agent to fill out the MLS Fact Sheet so that the appropriate data concerning your property can be properly entered into the MLS system. Refer to Appendix S-5.

Suffice it to say that it is very important that this Fact Sheet be filled out accurately and completely, because this form, like the Listing Agreement, requires the seller's signature. Therefore, the seller will be given the opportunity to go over the form carefully to be sure that the agent has the facts correct before signing.

The top portion, entitled KEYWORDS, requires that spaces be filled in as indicated. The (R) by most of the headings means that it is required by the computer that something be filled into that space. The format must be adhered to precisely or the computer simply will not accept it.

The middle section, entitled FEATURES, requires that the agent simply circle the appropriate features. In some categories only one feature can be circled while in others there might be several that apply.

The bottom section, entitled REMARKS, is the area where the agent has an opportunity to be a little creative and write an "ad" to his fellow brokers. Because I like to take some time with this portion of the Fact Sheet, I try to fill out as much of this as possible before I take it to the seller for his approval and signature.

Once these forms are completed, they should be entered into the system (usually direct via the office computer) at the earliest possible time.

YOUR INDIVIDUAL MARKETING BOOKLET

There are many questions that a prospective buyer and/or his agent will want to know about your property. It has been proven that the more readily this information is available, the more confident the buyer will be in making the decision to buy.

In this era of full disclosure, especially in California, the law has placed the onus squarely upon the seller to disclose anything adverse that he is aware of about the property. I believe, from a purely psychological point of view, that it is far better to present this information right up front, rather than to wait until the eleventh hour when the buyer is beginning to experience the normal buyer remorse syndromes.

With these thoughts in mind, I suggest to my clients that we prepare an individual marketing booklet, usually put together in a three-ring binder and left in the home for potential buyers and their agents to peruse. The following are items to be included in this marketing booklet:

Property Fact Sheet
Property Transfer Disclosure Statement
Pest Control Report
Covenants, Conditions, and Restrictions
    (CC&R's) (if applicable)
Special Study Zones Report (if applicable)
Soils or Structural Engineering Reports
    (if applicable)
Contractor's Inspection Report (if available)
Property Profile (from title company)
Plans for Alterations or Additions
    (if applicable)
Home Warranty Plan (if offered)
Special Equipment Report (Pools, Spas,
    Sprinkler & Alarm Systems, etc.)

8
The Purchase Contract

In Part One, the Purchase Contract & Receipt For Deposit was examined in detail. If you have not read that section or you need to refresh your memory, now would be the perfect time before we take a look at the Purchase Contract (Appendix B-1) from the seller's point of view.

When a seller is presented with an offer to purchase, he should be interested in three major aspects of the offer: 1) the net value of the offer, 2) the probability of the contract being consummated, and 3) the date that escrow will close.

THE NET VALUE OF THE OFFER

Obviously, the amount offered is the major aspect in the analysis of the economic value of the offer, but it is not the only aspect. What else besides title to the property is being requested for that price? Are items of personal property such as refrigerator, washer, or dryer expected to be included in the sale? If so, what are they worth to the seller? Is the property being bought "as is" or is the seller expected to bring certain things up to a stated standard? Termite repairs would be one example.

Is the seller being asked to carry back financing? If so, is the interest worth being without the funds?

Very often, the seller cannot afford to carry back, usually because he needs every dime he can get his hands on for another purchase.

Is the real estate commission as originally agreed upon? What closing costs will the seller face? The seller must look at net proceeds to determine whether or not this offer fulfills his reasons for selling in the first place. At this point you may find it helpful to refer to Appendix S-7: Checklist for Presentation of Offers.

REVIEWING THE CONTRACT'S CONTINGENCIES

Is this a clean offer, or is it so loaded with contingencies that it may never close? For instance, a contract contingent upon the sale of the buyer's present home may have doubtful value. To accept such an offer has the effect of taking your property off the market, although such agreements are usually accepted with the understanding that the property will continue to be offered for sale. If another acceptable offer comes along, it is generally worded so that the first offeror has seventy-two hours to remove the contingency or the seller is then free to sell to the second offeror without obligation to the first.

This sounds okay, except for one thing that many agents fail to inform their clients. The MLS rules usually state that if there is a pending sale or a kick-out clause (that is what we are talking about here), the listing must be revised to state as much. Most agents showing property to prospective buyers will avoid showing such properties because they are afraid the prospective buyers will fall in love with a property that they cannot have. Then they spend the next six months comparing everything they see to the one that got away. Except in terribly tight markets, most agents would simply prefer not to complicate life by opening up this particular can of worms. Therefore, even though the property is still actively on the market, in effect it really is not.

Continuing on the subject of contingencies, very few offers are totally free of them. During the period that they are in effect, you do not know for sure whether or not your property is sold. Because it is difficult to avoid contingencies altogether, the next best thing is to limit the amount of time that they remain in effect.

Physical inspections, approval of preliminary title reports, disclosures, and other documentation can be completed in ten to fourteen days. Any one of these gives the buyer a way out if he develops cold feet, and the longer time drags by, the more chance there is that this might occur.

The financing contingency, which is the most common contingency found in offers, cannot be resolved quite so quickly. Thirty days is the standard for this contingency. Certain aspects can be accomplished early on to assure that things don't wait until the last minute to come unglued because of this contingency.

First, the seller should carefully examine the terms of the financing upon which the contract is contingent. Are the terms reasonable for present market conditions? Refer to Financing Terms on page 52 of Part One. As you can see, the terms are very specifically spelled out. In the case of our example, the terms were quite reasonable for the prevailing market conditions. If you are presented with an offer that does not spell out the terms of the financing (and this happens a lot), or the terms are not readily attainable in current market conditions, then DO NOT ACCEPT THE OFFER AS IT STANDS. Otherwise, your property will be tied up without the slightest assurance that this contingency will be satisfied.

Next, if you will refer to Paragraph 1(H) of the Purchase Contract (Appendix B-1), you will note that this contract provides that the buyer must apply for financing within a specified period of time (in the case of our example, five days) and provide evidence of such to the seller. If this is not done, the seller has the option of rendering the contract null and void.

It is very important that this process get started immediately for several reasons. The sooner it gets started, the sooner it will be completed. The more you can keep the buyer's momentum going, the better the chance of combating the possibility of buyer's remorse setting in. Finally, get the buyer pre-qualified. Many smart buyers are going to a lender before they even find a home to buy and asking to be pre-qualified. They can usually get a letter from the lender stating that they have been pre-qualified for a loan up to specified limits. If this has not been done, insist that the bank qualify the buyer in a shorter period of time than thirty days. This can normally be done within ten days of receipt of the loan application.

Once you know that the buyer is qualified, the only thing left to worry about is the appraisal. Unless the property sold for significantly more than comparable properties have been selling, you can relax a little at this point.

I mentioned buyer remorse earlier, and I would like to discuss this in greater detail at this point. Almost everyone, no matter how new or how experienced at the home-buying game, goes through a period of serious doubt, or buyer's remorse, shortly after the transaction is ratified. This usually occurs within twenty-four to forty-eight hours after the deed is done.

Most buyers get through this period and carry on with great enthusiasm. A few, however, just don't make it. Fear takes over and the feeling never subsides. This person is going to find any excuse available to get out of the deal. This is an emotional problem and the best contracts in the world cannot protect against it. Fortunately, it usually occurs early on, so the property is normally not held off of the market for an protracted period of time.

As mentioned earlier in this section, nothing should be done to reinforce this very normal phenomenon. For instance, mandated disclosures or any negative facts that are bound to eventually surface should be made public before a contract is ever negotiated, when they can be dealt with during a period when the buyer does not feel threatened.

To provide such information shortly after a contract has been ratified very often hits the buyer at his absolute psychological low, and this unfortunate timing may be enough to kill the deal.

CLOSE OF ESCROW DATE

The final major concern of the seller should be the close of escrow date. Is the date convenient to future plans? Very often, he will be attempting to arrange for simultaneous closes for the home being sold and the one being bought. Frankly, I never cease to be amazed at how often we are able to make these work out.

Sometimes the seller will desire a quick close, other times a longer close. Very often I have seen a seller accept a lower offer which had a closing date more suitable to his needs. If you have an otherwise attractive offer, but the close date is unacceptable, then this is where a good dialogue between the two parties is essential. Preferably, this dialogue will be conducted through the agents involved, however, occasionally it makes sense to bring buyers and

sellers together and let them explain their needs to one another. This should never happen until all of the other aspects of the contract have been agreed upon.

If all parties are reasonable, a solution can usually be found. Of course, there are times when all parties are not reasonable or their various needs are simply not compatible. In such cases, you will simply have to wait until another buyer comes along.

MORE ABOUT CONTINGENCIES

We have already discussed contingencies and how they create uncertainties until they are removed. Let's take a brief look at the numerous contingencies that are often found in residential purchase contracts.

1) Contingent upon obtaining adequate financing: as stated before, this is standard and reasonable. Find out early on if the buyer is qualified and the terms are achievable.

2) Contingent upon pest control (or termite) inspection: this is standard in California and other areas where termites, beetles, dry rot, and other wood-destroying infections or infestations are prevalent. In my area of northern California, the inspection and report are provided by a licensed pest control contractor and paid for by the seller along with any work required to correct any unsatisfactory conditions found as a result of the inspection. The cost of these repairs can also be negotiated between seller and buyer. One note of caution: many mortgage lenders insist upon receiving a pest control clearance before funding the loan, thereby eliminating the possibility of the buyer taking the premises "as is" with the intent of correcting the problem at some future date. It is possible, however, if the buyer is planning extensive remodeling, for the lender to cooperate in some way so that the pest control work does not have to be completed up front.

3) Contingent upon further inspection of the property: again, a reasonable request. The buyer should be allowed to bring in contractors, engineers, and other selected experts to inspect the property to determine its structural integrity, the condition of the roof, plumbing, electrical system, furnace, appliances, septic system — just about anything he wants inspected. These inspections should be made at the buyer's expense and should be completed in a timely fashion. The seller has a right to copies of all written reports resulting from such inspections.

4) Contingent upon approval of preliminary title report: a preliminary title report is usually made available by the title company within a few days after escrow is opened. The buyer should examine this report very carefully. In it will be a legal description of the property and encumbrances against the property, including any easements of record. This could be important. The buyer may have been planning to build a swimming pool, and examination of the prelim shows an underground utility easement running right through the area where the pool would have gone. Again, get the contingency out of the way as quickly as possible.

5) Contingent upon the sale of another property: the other property is usually the buyer's present home. This is a fairly common but undesirable contingency from the seller's point of view.

Sometimes, however, it is very difficult to get the home sold without accepting such a contingency. The normal basis for accepting such a contingency is with a seventy-two hour kick-out clause. This clause states that the seller will continue to market the property while the buyer attempts to sell his present home. If another acceptable offer comes along before the buyer removes this contingency, then upon notification from the seller, the buyer has seventy-two hours to remove the contingency or their contract is null and void. Very often, the buyer simply cannot perform without the sale of his present property and therefore cannot remove

the contingency. The sale is voided and the backup offer moves into first position.

Sometimes this first buyer will then ask to be placed in second position behind the newly accepted offer in the hopes that the first position transaction falls through and in the meantime a buyer comes along for his house — a bit of a long shot, but sometimes it pays off. In any event, be sure that there is a time limit placed on this contingency.

Even with a kick-out clause, the contract should only remain subject to this contingency for a finite period of time. This period could run from thirty to ninety days or more, depending upon market conditions.

Before you, the seller, should even consider such a contingency, you should determine (usually through his agent) what the buyer's property is worth and what the asking price is or will be. In short, determine the marketability of the buyer's property before considering accepting a contingent sale. If there appears to be very little chance that the property will sell in a timely fashion, then it makes no sense for the seller to tie up the property in a contract that has very little chance of being fulfilled.

6) Contingent upon seller carrying some or all of the financing: this could be satisfied very quickly with a resounding NO!

There are advantages for some sellers in carrying back financing. If you do not have an immediate need for the funds, then you will want to invest them somewhere. A first mortgage on residential real estate is a sound investment that usually pays a better than average rate of return.

Before considering a carry back of any amount, check credit carefully. Do everything a bank would do. Order a credit report. Anyone can do it. Ask for employment verifications. Check references. Particularly check with a past mortgage holder or landlords. Remember, you may be asked to carry the financing because the buyer cannot get credit through the normal channels. If the banks do not want the loan, then neither do you.

Finally, before I would consider taking back financing, I would want to be sure that the buyer will be putting enough cash equity into the transaction so that there is little chance of defaulting. Otherwise, you might end up taking back a property that had been trashed to the point that it was no longer worth the amount owing to you.

7) Contingent upon seller finding the house of his choice: this is different! This time the contingency is in the contract to favor the seller rather than the buyer. This is sometimes used in a tight market where the seller would like to sell but is afraid of not finding another suitable home to buy. In such a market, it is difficult to buy contingent on the sale of a home because demand is high. Therefore, it makes sense to sell your home first, but make that sale contingent upon finding another home.

This is only appropriate in a strong seller's market where demand is high and available housing is in short supply. It is necessary that the buyer be willing and able to wait until the seller can find a home to buy. Again, a time limit must be placed on such a contingency. Thirty to ninety days would be appropriate depending upon the market.

OTHER ASPECTS OF THE PURCHASE CONTRACT

We will run through several areas of the Purchase Contract which have not yet been covered in this section.

Section 2: Fixtures and Personal Property

We could have a long discussion concerning what is real property and what is personal property. To keep it simple, real property is the land and anything permanently attached to it. Personal property is anything that is not real property. When you sell your home, you are presumed to be selling real property.

A built-in range or dishwasher is real property. A refrigerator, washer, and dryer are all personal property. They can be removed without doing damage in the process. In our area, window coverings are considered to be included with the sale unless otherwise specified. Anything can be included or not included as long as it is specifically stated and agreed upon in the contract. The test comes when nothing is stated in the contract and later there arises a difference of opinion as to whether an item is or is not included. The legal solution usually follows the line that if it qualifies as real property, then it is included. Otherwise, it is not included.

Paragraph 3(D): Risk of Loss

This is simple. As long as the seller is still the owner of record and still in possession, he bears the risk of loss in the case of damage or destruction of the premises. The buyer has the option to void the transaction and has the right to have returned any deposit or other expenses directly connected with the purchase of the property. This is only fair because the seller can no longer deliver what was contracted for.

Section 5: Transfer Disclosure

It became law as of January 1, 1987, in the state of California, that sellers of one to four family residences must provide a transfer disclosure statement on a form prescribed by the statute to the buyer within a specified time, or the buyer could rescind the contract at any time without suffering any loss. If the statement is provided within the specified time, then the buyer has a specified time during which he may rescind the contract. If he fails to act within the specified period, then his rights under this statute are lost.

The statement requires that the seller disclose anything negative about the building of which he is aware. This could include foundation problems, leaking roofs, faulty wiring, inoperable plumbing — anything.

The Real Estate Transfer Disclosure Statement (Appendix S-8) serves two purposes for the buyer. First, it gives him the knowledge to make an intelligent decision before it is too late. Second, it gives him evidence in the seller's own handwriting in the event that the seller lied and a lawsuit results.

This new law along with several landmark court decisions in California has placed the onus of responsibility squarely on the shoulders of the sellers. However, if this statement is filled out honestly up front and is accepted by the buyer, then it will actually serve to protect the seller from lawsuits in the future. The basic concept is a good one, and I expect to see similar court decisions in other states, and eventually a similar law requiring full disclosure.

Section 7: Time Is Of The Essence

This statement should be found somewhere in every purchase contract and means exactly what it says. Any dates missed without the full written consent of all parties to the contract could be grounds for rescinding the contract.

Section 9: Home Protection Plan

There are numerous companies such as American Home Shield that offer home protection plans which insure against failure of such items as the furnace, hot water heater, and built-in appliances.

The protection can be ordered by a simple phone call, costs between $250.00 and $350.00, and usually lasts for twelve months from close of escrow. There are quite a few exceptions to the coverage and each service call costs between $30.00 and $45.00.

Most of the time the plan does not pay off, however, on occasion a major expense, such as a new hot water heater or furnace problem, is covered and everyone concerned is very happy that the plan was in force.

From the seller's point of view, the plan serves two purposes. First, it is an inexpensive selling feature that sometimes impresses the potential buyer. The other advantage is that it provides one more piece of insurance against future liability. For these reasons, it is probably worth the price.

Section 10: Liquidated Damages

This states that in the event of a default by the buyer, the seller shall retain the deposit as his sole remedy as liquidated damages up to 3% of the purchase price.

The alternative is to go to court. Most agree that this is a poor alternative. I know that my several lawyer clients could not wait to initial the liquidated damages clause. I highly recommend that such a clause be incorporated in any purchase contract.

Section 14: Maintenance

This section simply says that it is the responsibility of the seller to maintain the property until close of escrow and transfer of possession, in at least as good condition as it was at the time the offer was made. It further states that the property shall be clean and free from seller's belongings and debris when title changes. Furthermore, buyer has the right just prior to close of escrow to perform a walk-through to be sure that this paragraph is being adhered to.

Section 16: Agency Disclosure

Theoretically, and by law, all agents have a fiduciary responsibility to the one who pays their commission, which is usually the seller. In practice, however, it does not really work that way. In California there is a strict new agency disclosure law that requires agents to disclose who is working for whom. An agent can be the listing agent (working for the seller) or the selling agent (working for the buyer, although the seller still pays the commission) or a dual agent (representing both seller and buyer). They are all legal as long as the relationship is disclosed. (See Appendix B-5.)

When you hire an agent to list your home for sale, you most likely will hire the one you feel will do the best job of getting your home sold. That is what it is all about. So it should be no surprise if that agent comes up with the buyer for your home. But at this point, particularly in California, the agent has a problem. He is now in a position of having to represent and counsel both parties to the same transaction. As such, he will undoubtedly become privy to confidential information, and there is great debate as to just how that information should be handled.

My advice is quite simple. Because there is some likelihood that your listing agent will end up in this very compromising situation, never quite bare your soul from day one. You can get all the advice in the world and you can explain what you are trying to accomplish with this sale, but never let the agent know your bottom line. Over the years, I've just seen too many listing agents making statements that compromise their client's bargaining position.

Finally, the law states that an agent must disclose if he has a personal interest (other than earning a commission) in any transaction in which he is acting as an agent. If an agent is trying to acquire your property either directly or through friends or relatives, there exists the strong possibility that this person knows something that you don't. It is quite possible that he is simply in the market for a house and likes yours, but chances are someone is trying to make a good deal at your expense.

Section 19: Offer and Acceptance

A. When the offer is made, it must be signed by the offeror to be valid. The offer must also state a specific date and time beyond which the offer is void.

B. The amount of the real estate commission is spelled out here and can be anything that has been agreed upon by or has been negotiated between the listing agent and seller.

C. This line, when initialled, indicates that the offer is being accepted SUBJECT TO A COUNTER-OFFER. If there is going to be a counter-offer, it is crucial to initial here, otherwise the signing of the offer could be construed to have been accepted as is.

D. This is where the offer is signed as accepted. It must be signed by all co-owners or it could be rendered invalid by any owner who did not sign.

CLOSE OF ESCROW — IT'S FINALLY SOLD

Once a contract has been ratified (fully accepted), there are quite a few things to accomplish before the close of escrow. Refer to Appendix S-9: Follow-Up During Escrow.

Most of these things are the buyer's responsibility, but it is important for the seller or the seller's agent to see to it that the buyer and/or his agent are resolving their responsibilities in a timely fashion.

The seller is responsible for providing a preliminary title report, providing any mandated disclosures, having a pest control inspection, getting any required damages repaired, and performing any other repairs or alterations required by any special terms of the purchase contract.

Occasionally, if some cloud, or defect, in title surfaces, it is the seller's responsibility to clear the title. This might involve acquiring a quit claim deed from an ex-spouse or making a neighbor remove an encroaching fence. Whatever the problem, it is the seller's responsibility to provide a good and marketable title, free of encumbrances except those agreed upon, to the buyer at time of closing.

Finally, when all contingencies have been removed, all financing and funding is in place, and an insurable title is available, a closing date will be set. In some parts of the country, the closing requires the coming together of all parties to the transaction, at which time the various documents are passed around for signatures, funds are disbursed, keys are turned over, and everyone shakes hands.

In California and many other states, closing involves a minimum of three days. First, the buyers and sellers each have a separate set of documents to sign, including loan documents for the buyer. Once these are signed, they are returned to the lender. The second day is for funding. The lender funds the loan. The title company prepares the final closing statements and cuts checks to the appropriate parties. On the third day the various documents are recorded and the funds are disbursed by the title company. This transaction is history!

MOVING ON

Depending on where you are going from here, several things may have happened as a result of this close of escrow. If you have bought another home, the funds from escrow may have been transferred to the other escrow in order to complete the transaction on your new home.

If you have not purchased another home, then you will probably walk away with a nice check burning a hole in your pocket. Before you go out and spend it all in one place, we had better talk about the potential tax consequences of the sale you have just completed.

When you sell your primary residence, the IRS expects you to pay a capital gain on the profit you made from the sale. This means the difference between the original purchase price plus any improvements (not repairs or maintenance) and the net selling price (selling price less commissions and other sales expenses). Never mind that most, if not all, of this difference came as a result of inflation, the IRS wants its share. At the present time, this capital gain is taxed at the same rate as your ordinary income.

Suppose you bought your home in 1959 for $25,000. Let's say you added a family room in 1963 for $5,000. Your basis would then be $30,000. Now let us suppose you sold the property in 1988 for $285,000. You paid a 6% real estate commission ($17,100) and had $400 in additional closing expenses. Your net from the sale would be $267,500. Your capital gain would be the difference between your net from the sale and your basis, or $237,500. Your present tax rate would most likely be either 28% or 33%. Using the lower of 28%, your tax liability on the sale of this property would be $66,500. That is heavy duty taxation.

Fortunately, there are two modifications to this law. First, if you buy another home equal to or greater in value than the net selling price of the one sold within twenty-four months of the close of escrow, the capital gain is deferred and carried forward.

Using the same example, suppose that within the twenty-four-month deadline, you bought another home for $275,000. This is more than the net selling price of your previous home, and therefore the capital gain is deferred. This does not mean that it is forgiven. It simply means that it is carried over until some future event, such as the sale of this new home, at which time it is added to any gain (or loss) that might result from the next transaction. Again, the sum of these gains (or losses) can be carried over once again if the same rules are followed.

If the next house that you buy costs less than the one previously sold, then some capital gain will be due, however, it will not be the full amount as described earlier. The IRS has a formula which reduces the capital gain based upon the purchase price of the new residence. The higher the purchase price of the new residence, the smaller the tax liability.

The second modification to this law takes place when one member of the household reaches the age of fifty-five. Once you reach this golden age, the IRS then forgives up to $125,000 of the accumulated capital gain that has accrued over the years.

You only get one shot at this $125,000 forgiveness of accumulated capital gain. For instance, let's say that you are over fifty-five and have an accumulated capital gain of $100,000 when you sell. You take advantage of the deduction and pay no capital gain. You rent for several years and then decide to buy another home. If, later on, you decide to sell that home, you cannot use the additional $25,000 you were unable to use the first time, since you may only elect to take this deduction once in your lifetime.

One warning: both the deference of capital gain and the one-time deduction only apply to your primary residence. These rules do not apply to vacation homes. Investment property is a whole different story.

As you can see, the tax laws of our land should have a significant bearing on a lifetime strategy of home ownership. The laws favor a strategy of buying as early as possible in adult life, parlaying upward from one home to another as economics dictate, and maintaining a continuous chain of home ownership until at least age fifty-five, at which time it might make the best sense to buy down to something more suitable to a retirement lifestyle and invest the $125,000 to help support that lifestyle. This is a strategy that has been followed successfully by millions of Americans.

If I have done my job properly, you now have the knowledge and understanding to adopt this or any other strategy in your pursuit of the Great American Dream. Do so with confidence.

Appendices

Glossary

ABSTRACT — A short legal history of a piece of property, tracing its ownership *(title)* through the years. An attorney or title insurance company reviews the abstract to make sure the title comes to a buyer free from any *defects* (problems).

ACCELERATION CLAUSE — A provision in a *mortgage* that may require the unpaid balance of the mortgage loan to become due immediately if the regular *mortgage payments* are not made, or if other terms of the mortgage are not met.

AGREEMENT OF SALE — *(see Purchase Agreement)*

AMORTIZATION — A payment plan by which the borrower reduces his debt gradually through monthly payments of *principal.*

APPRECIATION — An increase in the value of property.

APPRAISAL — An evaluation of a piece of property to determine its value; that is, what it would sell for in the marketplace.

ASSESSMENT — The value placed on property for purposes of taxation; may also refer to a special tax due for a special purpose, such as a sewer assessment.

ASSUMPTION OF MORTGAGE — The promise by the buyer of property to be legally responsible for the payment of an existing mortgage. The purchaser's name is substituted for the original *mortgagor's* (borrower's) name on the *mortgage note* and the original mortgagor is released from the responsibility of making the mortgage payments. Usually the lender must agree to an assumption.

BINDER — A simple contract between a buyer and a seller which states the basic terms of a offer to purchase property. It is usually good only for a limited period of time, until a more formal *purchase agreement* is prepared and signed by both parties. A small *deposit* of *earnest money* is made to "bind" the offer.

BROKER — *(see Real Estate Broker)*

CERTIFICATE OF TITLE — A document prepared by a title company or an attorney stating that the seller has a clear, marketable, and insurable title to the property he is offering for sale.

CLOSING — The final step in the sale and purchase of a property, when the title is transferred from the seller to the buyer; the buyer signs the mortgage, pays settlement costs; and any money due the seller or buyer is handed over.

CLOSING COSTS — Sometimes called Settlement Costs — costs in addition to the price of a house, usually including mortgage origination fee, title insurance, attorney's fee, and *prepayable* items such as taxes and insurance payments collected in advance and held in an *escrow* account.

CLOUD ON TITLE — *(see Title Defect)*

COMMISSION — Money paid to a real estate agent or broker by the seller as payment for finding a buyer and completing a sale. Usually it is a percentage of the sales price and is spelled out in the *purchase agreement.*

COMMUNITY PROPERTY — In some states, a form of ownership under which property acquired during a marriage is presumed to be owned jointly unless acquired as separate property of either spouse.

CONDITIONAL COMMITMENT — A promise to insure (generally with FHA loans) payment of a definite loan amount on a particular piece of property for a buyer with satisfactory credit.

CONDOMINIUM — Individual ownership of an apartment in a multi-unit project or development, and a proportionate interest in the common areas outside the apartment.

CONTRACTOR — A person or company who agrees to furnish materials and labor to do work for a certain price.

CONVENTIONAL LOAN — A mortgage loan which is *not* insured by *FHA* or guaranteed by *VA*.

COOPERATIVE — An apartment building or group of housing units owned by all the residents (generally a corporation) and run by an elected board of directors for the benefit of the residents. The resident lives in his unit but does *not* own it — he owns a share of stock in the corporation.

CREDIT RATING — A rating or evaluation made by a person or company (such as a Credit Bureau) based on one's present financial condition and past credit history.

CREDIT REPORT — A report usually ordered by a lender from a credit bureau to help determine a borrower's *credit rating*.

DEED — A written document by which the ownership of property is transferred from the seller (the *grantor*) to the buyer (the *grantee*).

DEED OF TRUST — In some states, a document used instead of a mortgage. It transfers title of the property to a *third party* (the trustee) who holds the title until the debt of mortgage loan is paid off, at which time the title (ownership) passes to the borrower. If the borrower defaults (fails to make payments), the trustee may sell the property at a public sale to pay off the loan.

DEED (QUITCLAIM DEED) — A deed which transfers only that title or right to a property that the holder of that title has at the time of the transfer. A quitclaim deed does not warrant (or guarantee) a clear title.

DEED (WARRANTY DEED) — A deed which guarantees that the title to a piece of property is free from any title defects.

DEFAULT — Failure to make mortgage payments on time, as agreed to in the *mortgage note* or *deed of trust*. If a payment is 30 days late, the mortgage is in default, and it may give the lender the right to start *foreclosure* proceedings.

DELINQUENCY — When a mortgage payment is past due.

DEPOSIT — A sum of money given to bind a sale of real estate — also called *earnest money*.

DEPRECIATION — A loss or decrease in the value of a piece of property due to age, wear and tear, or unfavorable changes in the neighborhood; opposite of *appreciation*.

DOCUMENTARY STAMPS — In some states a tax, in the form of stamps, required on deeds and mortgages when real estate *title* passes from one owner to another. The amount required differs from one state to another.

EARNEST MONEY — *(see Deposit)*

EASEMENT — The right to use land owned by another. For instance, the electric company has easement rights to allow their power lines to cross another's property.

ECOA — Equal Credit Opportunity Act — a federal law that requires lenders to loan without discrimination based on race, color, religion, national origin, sex, marital status, or income from public assistance programs.

ENCUMBRANCE — Anything that limits the interest in a title to property, such as a *mortgage,* a *lien,* an *easement,* a *deed restriction,* or unpaid taxes.

EQUITY — A buyer's initial ownership interest in a house that increases as he pays off a mortgage loan. When the mortgage is fully paid, the owner has 100% equity in his house.

ESCROW — Money or documents held by a third party until all the conditions of a contract are met.

ESCROW AGENT — The third party responsible to the buyer and seller or to the lender and borrower for holding the money or documents until the terms of a purchase agreement are met.

ESCROW PAYMENT — That part of a borrower's monthly payment held by the lender to pay for taxes, hazard insurance, mortgage insurance, and other items until they become due. Also known as impounds or reserves in some states.

FHA — Federal Housing Administration — a division of the U.S. Department of Housing and Urban Development *(HUD).* Its main activity is to insure home mortgage loans made by private lenders.

FmHA — Farmers Home Administration — a government agency (part of the Department of Agriculture) which provides financing to farmers or other qualified buyers (usually in rural areas) who are unable to obtain loans elsewhere.

FINANCE CHARGE — The total of all charges one must pay in order to get a loan.

FIRM COMMITMENT — An agreement from a lender to make a loan to a particular borrower on a particular property. Also an FHA or private mortgage insurance company agreement to insure a loan on a particular property for a particular borrower.

FORBEARANCE — The act of delaying legal action to *foreclose* on a mortgage that is overdue. Usually it is granted only when a satisfactory arrangement has been made with the lender to make up the late payments at a future date.

FORECLOSURE — The legal process by which a lender forces payment of a loan (under a *mortgage* or *deed of trust*) by taking the property from the owner *(mortgagor)* and selling it to pay off the debt.

GRANTEE — That party in the deed who is the buyer.

GRANTOR — That party in the deed who is the seller.

GUARANTEED LOAN — A loan guaranteed to be paid by the VA or FmHA in the event the borrower fails to do so *(defaults).*

GUARANTY — A promise by one party to pay the debt of another if that other fails to do so.

HAZARD INSURANCE — Insurance which protects against damage caused to property by fire, windstorm, or other common hazard. Required by many lenders to be carried in an amount at least equal to the mortgage.

HOMEOWNERS INSURANCE POLICY — Insurance that covers the house and its contents in the case of fire, wind damage, theft, and covers the homeowner in case someone is injured on the property and brings a suit.

HUD — The U.S. Department of Housing and Urban Development.

IMPOUND — *(see Escrow)*

INSTALLMENT — The regular payment that a borrower agrees to make to a lender.

INSURANCE BINDER — A document stating that an individual or property is insured, even though the insurance policy has not yet been issued.

INSURED LOAN — A loan insured by FHA or a private mortgage insurance company.

INTEREST — A charge paid for borrowing money. Also a right, share, or *title* in property.

JOINT TENANCY — An equal, undivided ownership of property by two or more persons. Should one of the parties die, his share of the ownership would pass to the surviving owners (right of survivorship).

LATE CHARGE — An additional fee a lender charges a borrower if his mortgage payments are not made on time.

LIEN — A hold or claim which someone has on the property of another, as *security* for a debt or charge; if a lien is not removed (if debt is not paid), the property may be sold to pay off the lien.

LISTING — Registering of properties for sale with one or more real estate brokers or agents allowing the broker who actually sells the property to get the *commission*.

LOAN DISCLOSURE NOTE — Document spelling out all the terms involved in obtaining and paying off a loan.

MORTGAGE — A special loan for buying property.

MORTGAGE INTEREST SUBSIDY — A monthly payment by the Federal Government to a mortgagee (lender) which reduces the amount of *interest* the mortgagor (homeowner) has to pay to the lender to as low as 4%, if the homeowner falls within certain income limits.

MORTGAGE ORIGINATION FEE — A charge by the lender for the work involved in the preparation and servicing of a mortgage request. Usually 1% of the loan amount.

MORTGAGEE — The lender who makes a mortgage loan.

MORTGAGOR — The person borrowing money for a mortgage loan.

OPTION (TO BUY) — An agreement granting a potential buyer the right to buy a piece of property at a stated price within a stated period of time.

PITI — Principal, interest, taxes, and insurance (in FHA and VA loans paid to the bank each month).

PLAT (OR PLOT) — A map of a piece of land showing its boundaries, length, width, and any easements.

POINT(S) — An amount equal to 1% of the principal amount of a loan. Points are a one-time charge collected by the lender at *closing* to increase the return on the loan. In FHA or VA loans, the borrower is not allowed to pay any points.

PREPAID ITEMS — An advance payment, at the time of closing, for taxes, hazard insurance, and mortgage insurance which is held in an *escrow account* by the lender.

PREPAYMENT PENALTY — A charge made by the lender if a mortgage loan is paid off *before* the due date. FHA does not permit such a penalty on its FHA-insured loans.

PRINCIPAL — The amount of money borrowed which must be paid back, along with interest and other finance charges.

PURCHASE AGREEMENT — A written document in which a seller agrees to sell, and a buyer agrees to buy a piece of property, with certain conditions and terms of the sale spelled out, such as sales price, date of closing, condition of property, etc. The agreement is secured by a *deposit* or down payment of *earnest money*.

QUITCLAIM DEED — *(see Deed, Quitclaim)*

REAL ESTATE — Land and the structures thereon. Also anything of a permanent nature such as trees, minerals, and the interest and rights in these items.

REAL ESTATE AGENT — An individual who can show property for sale on behalf of a seller, but who may not have a license to transact the sale and collect the sales commission.

REAL ESTATE BROKER — An individual who can show property for sale on behalf of a seller, and who has a valid license to sell real estate. The real estate broker represents the seller and is paid a *commission* when the property is sold.

REALTOR — A real estate broker or an associate holding active membership in a local and real estate board affiliated with the National Association of Realtors.

RECORDING FEES — The charge by an attorney to put on public record the details of legal documents such as a deed or mortgage.

REFINANCING — The process of paying off one loan with the money (proceeds) from another loan.

RESPA — Real Estate Settlement Procedures Act — A federal law that requires lenders to send to the home mortgage borrower (within *3* business days) an estimate of the *closing (settlement) costs*. RESPA also limits the amount lenders may hold in an *escrow* account for real estate taxes and insurance, and requires the disclosure of settlement costs to both buyers and sellers 24 hours before the *closing*.

RESTRICTIONS — A legal limitation in the deed on the use of property.

RIGHT OF RESCISSION — That section of the Truth-in-Lending Law which allows a consumer the right to change his/her mind and cancel a contract within 3 days after signing it. This right to cancel is in force if the contract would involve obtaining a loan, and the loan would place a *lien* on the property.

RIGHT OF WAY — An *easement* on property, where the property owner gives another person the right to pass over his land.

SALES AGREEMENT — *(see Purchase Agreement)*

SETTLEMENT COSTS — *(see Closing Costs)*

SOLE OWNER — Ownership of a property by a single individual.

STAMPS — *(see Documentary Stamps)*

SURVEY — A map or *plat* made by a licensed surveyor showing the measurements of a piece of land; its location, dimensions, and the location and dimensions of any improvements on the land.

TENANCY-BY-THE-ENTIRETY — The joint ownership of property by a husband and wife. If either one dies, his or her share of ownership goes to the survivor.

TENANCY-IN-COMMON — When property is owned by two or more persons with the terms creating a *joint tenancy*. In the event one of the owners dies, his share of the property would not go to the other owner automatically, but rather to his heirs.

TITLE — The rights of ownership of a particular property, and the documents which proves that ownership (commonly a *deed*).

TITLE DEFECTS — An outstanding claim or *encumbrance* on property which affects its marketability (whether or not it can be freely sold).

TITLE INSURANCE — Special insurance which usually protects lenders against loss of their interest in property due to legal defects in the title. An owner can protect his interest by purchasing separate coverage.

TITLE SEARCH — An examination of public records to uncover any past or current facts regarding the ownership of a piece of property. A title search is intended to make sure the title is marketable and free from *defects*.

TRUTH-IN-LENDING — A federal law which provides that the terms of a loan (including all the finance charges) must be disclosed to the borrower before the loan is signed. It also contains a provision for the *Right of Recission*.

VA — *Veterans Administration* — The VA guarantees a certain proportion of a mortgage loan made to a veteran by a private lender. Sometimes called GI loans, these usually require very low down payments and permit long repayment terms.

WARRANTY DEED — *(see Deed, Warranty)*

ZONING — The power of a local municipal government (city or town) to regulate the use of property within the municipality.

From: *Homebuyer's Information Package.*
U.S. Department of Housing and Urban Development
Office of Policy Development and Research

REGIONAL DATA SERVICE
REAL ESTATE PURCHASE CONTRACT AND RECEIPT FOR DEPOSIT
This is more than a receipt for money. This is intended to be a legally binding contract. Read it carefully.

MENLO PARK ,California _MARCH 22_ ,19 _89_

RECEIVED FROM _ROBERT C. & PATRICIA H. MOORE, HUSBAND & WIFE_ herein called "Buyer"
the sum set forth in "1.A" below as a deposit on account of the purchase price of _THREE HUNDRED,_
FIFTY-FIVE THOUSAND _____ (Dollars) (\$ _355,000.00_)
for the purchase of property situated in _SAN CARLOS_ County of _SAN MATEO_ .
State of California, described as follows _850 EXETER AVENUE_
upon the following terms and conditions:

1. FINANCING TERMS

A. DEPOSIT evidenced by ☒ personal check, ☐ cash, ☐ cashier's check, ☐ other: _____
_____ which shall be held uncashed until acceptance, at
which time it shall be deposited in Escrow Holder's or Broker's trust account within _3_ calendar
days. .... \$ _2,000_

B. ADDITIONAL DEPOSIT to be deposited to Escrow Holder or Broker's Trust Account in the form
of _PERSONAL CHECK_ on or before _SATISFACTION OF ALL_
CONTINGENCIES (See paragraph 10 regarding LIQUIDATED DAMAGES.) \$ _8,650_

C. BALANCE OF CASH DOWN PAYMENT to be deposited with Escrow Holder prior to the close
of escrow. .... \$ _43,100_

D. ☒ NEW FIRST Deed of Trust, or ☐ ASSUMPTION of Existing First Deed of Trust; encumbering
subject property securing a note payable to ☒ Lender ☐ Seller at approximately
\$ _2047.23_ per month to include: ☒ principal and interest, ☐ interest only,
☐ _____, at no more than _8½_ % ☐ fixed, ☒ _ADJUSTABLE_ interest per annum,
for no less than _30_ years, with an interest rate cap of _13½_ %. ☒ Buyer,
☐ _____, to pay loan fee not to exceed _2_ % of loan.
☐ RDS Finance Addendum (Seller Carryback) .... \$ _266,250_

E. ☒ NEW SECOND Deed of Trust, or ☐ ASSUMPTION of Existing Second Deed of Trust;
encumbering the subject property securing a note payable to ☐ Lender ☒ Seller at
approximately \$ _291.67_ per month, to include: ☐ principal and interest, ☒ interest
only, ☐ _____, at no more than _10_ % ☒ fixed, ☐ _____, interest per
annum, for no less than _5_ years with an interest rate cap of _____%. ☐ Buyer,
☐ _____, to pay loan fee not to exceed_____ % of loan, ☒ RDS Finance
addendum (Seller Carryback). .... \$ _35,000_

F. OTHER FINANCING TERMS: _____
_____
_____
_____
_____
_____ \$ _____

G. TOTAL PURCHASE PRICE, not including closing costs. .... \$ _355,000_

H. LOAN APPLICATION: Buyer will apply for the above financing within _5_ calendar days of acceptance. Buyer shall provide
seller evidence of loan application within the above time limit.

I. FINANCING CONTINGENCY TERMS: This contract is subject to and conditioned upon Buyer obtaining financing. Buyer to
qualify for and obtain financing or loan commitments on the terms set forth above. Buyer to remove this contingency in writing in
accordance with the provisions of paragraph 8.

J. EXISTING ENCUMBRANCES CONTINGENCY: If Buyer is to assume, or purchase "subject to", any of the loans of record, Seller,
within _____ calendar days of acceptance, shall provide Buyer with copies of all applicable notes, deeds of trust, current interest
rates and balances. Buyer shall notify Seller in writing of Buyer's approval or disapproval of the terms of the notes and deeds of
trust encumbering the property and shall remove this contingency in accordance with the provisions of paragraph 8. Buyer shall
not unreasonably withhold approval. Buyer and Seller acknowledge that the existing loans encumbering the property may
contain a clause that provides said loans are "due-on-sale" of the property. Seller shall pay any prepayment penalty that may be
imposed on any existing loans payable on close of escrow. Buyer shall pay any prepayment penalty which may become due after
close of escrow on any loans assumed or taken "subject to". Any net differences between the approximate balances of loans
shown above, which are to be assumed, and the actual balances of said loans at close of escrow shall be:

□ paid in cash, □ other _____ .

The impound account of any loan assumed or taken "subject to" shall be charged to Buyer, without deficiency or shortage, and credited to Seller in escrow.

2. FIXTURES AND PERSONAL PROPERTY

A. FIXTURES: Permanently installed light and plumbing fixtures, wall to wall carpeting, other attached floor coverings, window coverings (including hardware), existing window and door screens in present condition, awnings, pool and spa equipment, water softener system, air conditioners for which special openings have been made, built in appliances, solar system(s), alarm system(s), television antenna(s), mailbox, unpotted outdoor plants and trees, attached fireplace screens, garage door openers and transmitters and items permanently attached to the real property are included if presently installed.

FIXTURES NOT INCLUDED: _NONE_ _____
_____

B. PERSONAL PROPERTY TO BE INCLUDED: The following items of personal property, free of liens and without warranty of condition, are included:

REFRIGERATOR, WASHER, DRYER _____
_____
_____

BUYERS' INITIALS: (_RCM_) (_RHM_)   SELLERS' INITIALS: (_____) (_____)

Subject Property Address: _850 EXETER AVENUE, SAN CARLOS_

3. CONDITIONS RELATING TO TITLE:

A. TITLE DOCUMENTS: Buyer to be provided with current Preliminary Report, CC&R's, Homeowners' Association Bylaws, Rules and Regulations, if any. This contract is contingent upon Buyer's written approval of these documents in accordance with the provisions of Paragraph 8.

B. BONDS & ASSESSMENTS: If applicable, the amount of Bonds or Assessments for any Public Improvements shall be ASSUMED BY BUYER. This contract is contingent upon Buyer's written approval of Bonds & Assessments. This contingency shall be removed in accordance with provisions of Paragraph 8.

C. TITLE: Title is to be free of liens, encumbrances, easements, restrictions, rights and conditions of record or known to Seller, other than the following: (a) Current property taxes, (b) covenants, conditions, restrictions and public utility easements of record, if any, provided the same do not adversely affect the continued use of the property for the purposes for which it is presently being used, and (c) (unrecorded items that effect title) _____
Buyer to be provided at _BUYER'S_ _____ expense a Standard California Land Title Association Policy issued by _FIRST AMERICAN TITLE_ Company, showing title vested in Buyer subject only to the above. If Seller is unwilling or unable to eliminate any title matter disapproved by Buyer as above, or if Seller fails to deliver title as above, Buyer may terminate this agreement. In any case, the deposit shall be returned to Buyer.

Escrow fee to be paid by _BUYER_ _____.

D. RISK OF LOSS: If the improvements on said property are destroyed or materially damaged prior to transfer of title, then at the option of the Buyer, the deposit shall be released to Buyer. Any other sums paid by Buyer for credit reports, appraisals and property inspections of any kind shall be reimbursed to Buyer by Seller and Seller shall pay all expenses incurred in connection with examination of title. If loss is covered by insurance, Buyer may at his option complete the purchase and Seller shall assign any existing insurance proceeds covering said loss to Buyer.

E. REASSESSMENT DISCLOSURE: Buyer and Seller are aware that the property will be reassessed upon change of ownership. A supplemental tax bill will be received after close of escrow, which may reflect an increase or decrease in taxes based on property value. If there is an impound for taxes with a lender, the amount of the periodic impound may change. Buyer will be required to complete "Preliminary Change of Ownership Report" prior to recording of the deed. (Revenue and Taxation Code 480.3).

4. ADDENDA:

Any addenda checked below which are ATTACHED hereto and signed by the Buyer and Seller shall be deemed part of this agreement.
☐ Condominium/PUD Disclosure   ☐ Res. Lease Agreement after Sale (Seller in possession)
☐ Contingency Release Clause   ☐ _____
☒ RDS Finance Addendum (Seller Carryback)   ☐ _____
☐ Interim Occupancy Agreement (Buyer in possession)   ☐ _____
                                                    ☐ _____

5. TRANSFER DISCLOSURE:

A. Unless exempt, Seller, shall comply with Civil Code Sections 1102 et seq., by providing Buyer with a fully completed Real Estate Transfer Disclosure Statement (TDS) signed by Seller, Agent representing Seller, and Agent obtaining the offer:
1) ☐ Buyer has received and read a Real Estate Transfer Disclosure Statement; or
2) ☒ Seller shall provide Buyer with a fully completed Real Estate Transfer Disclosure Statement within _3_ calendar days of Seller's acceptance.   Buyer shall have three (3) days after delivery to Buyer, in person, or five (5) days after delivery by deposit in the mail, to terminate this agreement by delivery of a written notice of termination to Seller or Seller's Agent.

B. ALTERATIONS: Seller is obligated under California Law to disclose to Buyer any additions or alterations made by Seller, or known to Seller, without the benefit of appropriate government permits and final approvals. Seller shall also disclose notices of violations of any city, county, state, federal, building, zoning, fire, or health codes ordinances.

6. MANDATED DISCLOSURES:

When applicable to the property, Seller shall provide Buyer at Seller's expense the following information in writing as mandated by law. This contract is contingent upon Buyer's written approval of items A, B, and C (Below). Items D, E, F and G, are mandated disclosures but not contingencies. Buyer shall remove this contingency in accordance with the provisions of Paragraph 8.

A. GEOLOGICAL HAZARDS: Identified as SPECIAL STUDY ZONES, and other high risk areas. [Ref. Calif. Public Resources Code 2621-2625; Santa Clara County Ordinance C12-645, C12-647 & C12-650; City of San Jose Municipal Code Section 17.10.020 (H)].

B. HUD FLOOD HAZARD ZONE and lenders requirements for HUD Flood Insurance.

C. **CONDOMINIUM/PUD** (Common Interest Subdivision): California Civil Code Sec. 1365 and 1368. See RDS Addendum.

D. **SMOKE DETECTORS:** As required by law, smoke detector(s) shall be installed at the expense of Seller, prior to the close of escrow, and a compliance report obtained if required by local ordinances.

E. **SELLER FINANCING DISCLOSURE STATEMENT:** California Civil Code Sec. 2956-2967.

F. **TAX WITHHOLDING:** Under the Foreign Investment in Real Property Tax Act (FIRPTA), IRC 1445, unless an exemption applies, every Buyer of U.S. real property must, deduct and withhold from Seller's proceeds ten percent (10%) of the gross sales price. The primary exemptions are: No withholding is required if (a) Seller provides Buyer with an affidavit under penalty of perjury, that Seller is not a foreign person", or (b) Seller provides Buyer with a "qualifying statement" issued by the Internal Revenue Service, or (c) if Buyer purchases real property for use as a residence and the purchase price is $300,000.00 or less and if Buyer or a member of Buyer's family has definite plans to reside at the property for at least 50% of the number of days it is in use during each of the first two twelve-month periods after transfer. Seller and Buyer agree to execute and deliver as directed any instrument, affidavit and statement, or to perform any act reasonably necessary to carry out the provisions of the FIRPTA and regulations promulgated thereunder.

G. **ENERGY AUDIT & COMPLIANCE FORM.**

H. **OTHER** _____
_____

_____

BUYERS' INITIALS: (_RCM_)   (_RHM_)   SELLERS' INITIALS: (_____)   (_____)

Subject Property Address: _850 EXETER AVENUE, SAN CARLOS_

7. TIME: TIME IS OF THE ESSENCE IN THIS CONTRACT. Extensions, if any, must be agreed to in writing by all parties.

8. CONTINGENCY REMOVAL: IN THE EVENT ALL CONTINGENCIES ARE NOT REMOVED IN WRITING WITHIN THE AGREED UPON TIMES, THIS CONTRACT, AT THE OPTION OF THE SELLER, MAY BE NULL AND VOID.

THE FOLLOWING CONTINGENCIES IF APPLICABLE ARE TO BE REMOVED IN WRITING WITHIN THE AGREED UPON TIMES.

A. Financing Contingency (Para. 1.I.) shall be removed on or before _30_ calendar days from acceptance.

B. Title Documents (Para. 3.A.)
Mandated Disclosures (Para. 6)
Condition of Property (Para. 13.A.)
Condominium/PUD (Para. 6.C.)
RDS Finance Addendum (Seller Carryback)
(Para. 1.D. and 4.)
Existing Encumbrances Contingency (Para.1.J.)
Bonds and Assessments (Para. 3.B.)
Other Contingencies Set Forth Here:

Shall be removed _14_ Calendar days from acceptance.

☐ _____
☐ _____
☐ _____

9. HOME PROTECTION PLAN: Buyer and Seller have been informed that Home Protection Plans are available. Such plans may provide additional protection and benefit to a Seller or Buyer. The Broker(s) in this transaction do not endorse or approve any particular company or program.

A. WAIVED: By placing their initials here, Buyer and Seller elect not to purchase a Home Protection Plan.
BUYERS' INITIALS: (_LCM_) (_RHM_)　　　　SELLER'S INITIALS: (_____) (_____)

B. ACCEPTANCE: A Home Protection Plan shall be issued by _____ Company at a cost not to exceed $ _____ which shall be paid by _____ .

10. LIQUIDATED DAMAGES:

A. **IF BUYER FAILS TO COMPLETE THE PURCHASE AS HEREIN PROVIDED, BY REASON OF ANY DEFAULT OF BUYER, SELLER SHALL BE RELEASED FROM HIS OBLIGATION TO SELL THE PROPERTY TO BUYER AND MAY PROCEED AGAINST BUYER UPON ANY CLAIM OR REMEDY WHICH HE MAY HAVE IN LAW OR EQUITY; PROVIDED, HOWEVER, THAT BY PLACING THEIR INITIALS HERE BUYER (_LCM_) (_RHM_), SELLER (_____) (_____) AGREE THAT SELLER SHALL RETAIN THE DEPOSIT AS HIS SOLE REMEDY AS LIQUIDATED DAMAGES. IF THE PROPERTY IS A DWELLING WITH NOT MORE THAN FOUR UNITS, ONE OF WHICH THE BUYER INTENDS TO OCCUPY AS HIS RESIDENCE, SELLER SHALL RETAIN AS LIQUIDATED DAMAGES THE DEPOSIT ACTUALLY PAID, OR ANY AMOUNT THEREFROM, NOT MORE THAN 3% OF THE PURCHASE PRICE AND PROMPTLY RETURN ANY EXCESS TO BUYER. THE ABOVE 3% LIMITATION DOES NOT APPLY IF THE BUYER DOES NOT INTEND TO OCCUPY THE PROPERTY AS HIS RESIDENCE.**

B. **THE BUYER ☐ DOES, ☐ DOES NOT INTEND TO OCCUPY THE PROPERTY AS HIS RESIDENCE.**

C. **IF THE BUYER AND SELLER HAVE INITIALED THE LIQUIDATED DAMAGES AGREEMENT IN PARAGRAPH 10.A., THEY ALSO AGREE TO EXECUTE, AT THE TIME OF ANY INCREASE IN DEPOSIT, A C.A.R. FORM RID-11, "RECEIPT FOR INCREASE OF DEPOSIT", OR SIMILAR TYPE FORM, WHICH REITERATES THE LIQUIDATED DAMAGES PROVISION.**

11. STRUCTURAL PEST CONTROL CERTIFICATION:

A. Within ___14___ calendar days after the acceptance of this contract, the ☐ Buyer, ☒Seller shall provide at ☐Buyer's, ☒Seller's expense a current written report of an inspection, by a licensed Structural Pest Control Operator. This report shall include the main building and all attached structures.

The following detached structures to be included:_____

_____

_____

B. If no infestation of wood destroying pests or organisms is found, the report shall include a CERTIFICATION in accordance with Business & Professions (B & P) Code 8519(a).

C. All work recommended in said report to repair damages caused by infestation or infection of wood destroying pests or organisms shall be done by a licensed contractor at the expense of the Seller in compliance with all applicable codes, and with good workmanship and with materials of comparable quality including repair of any leaking shower(s), repairs of other water leakage and to correct condition(s) which have caused damage. Funds for said work to be performed shall be held in escrow and disbursed upon receipt of the latter of: close of escrow; a CERTIFICATION on the "Notice of Work Completed"; or on a reinspection by the licensed pest control operator to provide, in accordance with B&P Code 8519(b), a certification that, "the property described herein is now free of active infestation or infection."

D. Buyers agree that any work to correct conditions usually deemed likely to lead to infestation of wood-destroying pests or organisms, but where no evidence of existing infestation or infections found with respect to such conditions, is NOT the responsibility of the Seller and that such work shall be done only if requested by Buyer and then at the expense of Buyer.

BUYERS' INITIALS: (_RCM_)   (_RXM_)   SELLERS' INITIALS: (_____)   (_____)

Page 3 of 5

Subject Property Address: _850 Exeter Avenue, San Carlos_

E. If inspection of inaccessible area is recommended in the report, Buyer has the option of accepting and approving the report or requesting further inspection be made at the Buyer's expense. If further inspection is made prior to close of escrow and infestation, infection, or damage is found, repair of such damage and all work to correct conditions caused by infestation or damage, and the cost of entry and closing of the inaccessible area shall be at the expense of the Seller. If no infestation, infection, or damage is found, the cost of entry and closing of the inaccesible area a shall be at the expense of Buyer. Seller consents to such an inspection and acknowledges his responsibility under Civil Code Section 1099 to deliver to Buyer a copy of the INSPECTION REPORT, A "NOTICE OF WORK COMPLETED" or a "CERTIFICATION pursuant to B&P Code 8519" as may be required as soon as practical before transfer of title or the execution of a real property sales contract as defined in Civil Code Section 2985. Seller directs Listing Broker to deliver such copies of the above document as may be required. Any changes to the above terms to be noted in Paragraph 16. If inaccessibility is caused by Sellers personal property then Seller, at Seller's expense, shall authorize reinspection prior to close of escrow.

Seller shall not be responsible for any expense related to infestation, infection or damage which has not been disclosed to Seller in writing prior to close of escrow.

F. In the absence of any written agreement to the contrary between Buyer and Seller all repairs to be completed prior to close of escrow.

12. LEGAL NATURE OF AGREEMENT:

A. ENTIRE AGREEMENT: This writing expresses the entire agreement of the parties. There are no other representations, oral or written which in any manner alter the applicable clauses and conditions of this contract.

B. BINDING AGREEMENT: This agreement is binding upon the heirs, executors, administrators, successors and assigns of the Buyer and Seller, and shall survive the recordation of Grant Deed and close of escrow. Buyer may not assign his rights hereunder without prior written consent of Seller.

C. ARBITRATION: If the only controversy or claim between the parties arises out of or relates to the disposition of the Buyer's deposit, such controversy or claim SHALL be decided by binding arbitration in accordance with the Rules of the American Arbitration Association, and judgment upon the award rendered by the arbitrator(s) may be entered in any court having jurisdiction thereof. The provisions of Code of Civil Procedure Section 1283.05 shall be applicable to such arbitration.

D. ATTORNEY FEES: In the event any legal or equitable action, arbitration or proceeding between the buyer, seller and/or their agents/brokers arising out of this agreement, the prevailing party, Buyer, Seller, Broker/Agent shall be awarded reasonable attorney's fees and court or arbitration costs in addition to any other judgment or award.

E. DISSEMINATION OF INFORMATION: All parties authorize Brokers to disseminate information concerning sales price, terms and financing of this transaction after recording.

13. CONDITION OF PROPERTY:

A. This contract is contingent upon and subject to Buyers approval of the condition of the property. Buyer shall have the right and opportunity at Buyer's sole and complete expense to select licensed contractors and/or other qualified professionals to inspect and investigate the subject property including, but not limited to, the foundation, roof, heating, electrical, plumbing, septic tank, drain fields, air conditioning, pool, spa, hot tub, presence of any health hazards (including, but not limited to asbestos, radon gas, formaldehyde & other toxic substances), soils and geological conditions, boundary lines, set backs, compliance with zoning ordinance, building codes or any other factor which may affect the value or desirability of the property. No inspections may be made by any building department inspector or government employee without the prior written approval of Seller. Buyer warrants that Buyer will keep the subject property free and clear of any liens and indemnify and hold the Seller harmless from any liability claims, demands, damages, or costs and repair all damages to the property arising from any and all of the inspections mentioned above. Seller shall make the property reasonably available for such inspections. Buyer shall furnish at no cost to Seller copies of all reports concerning the property obtained by Buyer within the time frame of this paragraph. If the Buyer finds any deficiencies not covered under the normal maintenance in Paragraph 14 that are reasonably unsatisfactory to the Buyer, then the Buyer may cancel this contract or remove the contingency in accordance with Paragraph 8.

THE REAL ESTATE BROKER(S) AND AGENTS INVOLVED in this transaction do not encourage or recommend a waiver of this right to inspection. The Real Estate Broker(s) and Agents in this transaction further recommend and encourage the Buyer to obtain insurance coverage for any potential problems with regard to the physical condition of the property. In the event of waiver of the right of inspection, Buyer agrees that the Real Estate Broker(s) and Agents and Seller shall be free of any liability and claims for damages and Buyers will save and hold harmless Sellers and the Real Estate Broker(s) and Agents involved in this transacation from any and all liability, loss, costs or obligation on account of or arising out of the damages subsequently discovered by Buyer or their Agents.

B. Buyer understands subject property is approximately _4_ years old and should not be expected to meet the same expectations as a new property.

C. Assuming a representation of square footage has been made, Buyer understands and agrees that said representation is only an approximation of the exact number of square feet the property contains. The Buyer has the right to obtain his own measurement of square footage.

14. MAINTENANCE

A. THE FOLLOWING SYSTEMS ARE TO BE IN GOOD WORKING ORDER UNTIL BUYER TAKES POSSESSION: (1) Heating, cooling, plumbing, built-in appliances, pool, attached pool equipment, and spa, solar, electrical, sprinklers, alarm, sewer, and any other mechanical system presently installed on property. (2) Roof to be free of leaks. (3) Broken or cracked glass to be replaced. ANY EXCEPTIONS TO THIS PARAGRAPH MUST BE AGREED UPON BY BUYERS AND SELLERS IN WRITING PRIOR TO ACCEPTANCE AND MADE A PART OF THIS CONTRACT.

B. Until Buyer's possession, Seller shall maintain the remainder of property (all buildings, grounds and landscaping) in the same general condition as date of acceptance. By possession date, property to be cleaned and free of all personal belongings and debris.

C. Should labor or materials be required to comply with any repair provisions of this contract, Seller agrees that all work shall be performed using good workmanship and with materials of comparable quality, in compliance with applicable Codes and Permits (where required) and completed prior to Close of Escrow. Seller shall allow Buyer to reinspect property prior to Close of Escrow, to affirm Seller(s) compliance with the repair provisions of this contract.

D. Buyer and Seller understand the Broker(s) is not responsible for Sellers performance under this Paragraph and Brokers shall, in no way, be liable for any breach of it's provisions by the Seller.

15. KEYS: Seller shall, at close of escrow, provide Buyer with keys and/or means to operate all property locks and alarms, if any.

BUYERS' INITIALS: (*LCM*) (*RHM*)   SELLERS' INITIALS: (_____)   (_____)

COPYRIGHT © 1988, REGIONAL DATA SERVICE

5/88   *Page 4 of 5*

Subject Property Address: _850 EXETER AVENUE, SAN CARLOS_

16. AGENCY DISCLOSURE: (As required by the Civil Code.)

 A. BUYER AND SELLER ACKNOWLEDGE PRIOR RECEIPT OF THE AGENCY DISCLOSURE FORMS.

 B. AGENCY CONFIRMATION: the following agency relationship(s) are hereby confirmed for this transaction.

 LISTING AGENT: _SMITH REALTY_   SELLING AGENT: _LOWELL HODGKINS & ASSOCS._

 is the agent of (check one):   (if not the same as Listing Agent)

 ☒ the Seller exclusively; or   is the agent of (check one): ☐ the Seller exclusively; or

 ☐ both the Buyer and Seller   ☒ the Buyer exclusively; or ☐ both the Buyer and Seller

 NOTE: Listing Agent refers to Listing Firm. Selling Agent refers to Selling Firm.

17. OTHER TERMS AND CONDITIONS: _____

_____

_____

_____

_____

_____

_____

18. ESCROW CONDITIONS AND INSTRUCTIONS:

 A. CLOSE OF ESCROW: Transfer of title/recording shall be on _MAY 22, 1989_ (date). Any change in this date must have mutual written consent of Buyer and Seller.

 B. POSSESSION: Possession of the property shall be delivered to Buyer: ☒ noon on date or recording, ☐ not later than _____ days after the date of recording, or ☐ _____.

 In the event Seller does not deliver possession to Buyer at the date specified then, Seller shall be liable to Buyer for all damages, including consequential damages Buyer has sustained as occasioned by the delay.

 C. PRORATIONS: Taxes for the fiscal year, interest on any loan assumed by Buyer, homeowners association dues, rents and premiums on insurance acceptable to Buyer shall be prorated: ☒ from date of recording; ☐ _____.

 D. TRANSFER TAXES: Seller shall pay the cost of county real property transfer tax. Transfer taxes or fees required by any other lawful authority shall be paid by _SELLER_ .

 E. RELEASE OF FUNDS: Funds placed in the Trust Account of either Broker or Escrow Holder will not be released automatically. A release is required prior to any disbursement signed by all the parties including Brokers.

 F. ESCROW INSTRUCTIONS: This paragraph, as well as Paragraph 19.B., together with any additional escrow instructions shall constitute joint escrow instructions to the escrow holder. The parties shall execute such additional escrow instructions as requested by the escrow holder not inconsistent with the provisions of Paragraphs 18 and 19 herein. Nothing in this paragraph shall impose any duty upon the escrow holder to concern itself with other provisions of this contract nor to make any determination as to the ownership of or right, title or interest in any funds deposited in the event of any alleged failure of performance by either Buyer or Seller. The Buyer and Seller acknowledge that they have been informed that the use of certain out of state funds and use of drafts may cause a delay of up to ten (10) days in closing of the escrow.

19. OFFER AND ACCEPTANCE:

 A. This constitutes an offer to purchase the described property and shall be deemed revoked unless accepted in writing by Seller by _3/23/89 – 10:00 P.M._ (date/time) and such acceptance is so communicated to Buyer or Buyer's Agent. Buyer shall receive a signed copy hereof as soon after Seller's acceptance as practical. Buyer hereby acknowledges receipt of a copy of this agreement.

 Date _3-22-89_ Buyer _Robert C. Moore_

 Date _3/22/89_ Buyer _Patricia H. Moore_

 Date _____ Selling Office _LOWELL HODGKINS & ASSOCS._ By: _Lowell R. Hodgkins_

 Address _581 MARLIN COURT_   Telephone _555-5661_
 REDWOOD CITY, CA 94065

 B. BROKERAGE FEE: In consideration of services rendered, Seller agrees to pay Listing and Selling Broker a brokerage fee in the sum of _____ (or) _6_ % of the sale price, and Seller hereby assigns to Listing Broker said amount from the proceeds of this sales transaction and irrevocably instructs Escrow Holder to disburse said sums to Listing and Selling Broker at the time of close of escrow. If the sale to Buyer is prevented by any default of Seller, said fee shall be due and payable at the time of such default. If the sale is prevented by any default of Buyer, said fee shall be due and payable if and when Seller collects damages from Buyer by suit or otherwise, and then in an amount equal to the lesser of such commission, or one half (½) of the damages collected after deducting all expenses of collection. Not withstanding the above, the mutual recission of this agreement by Buyer and Seller shall not relieve said parties of their obligations to Broker herein. In any action between Broker and Seller arising out of this agreement, the prevailing party shall be entitled to reasonable attorney's fees and costs.

Listing Broker hereby assigns to Selling Broker the amount of _____
(or) _____9____% of the sales price from said brokerage fee and instructs Escrow Holder to disburse said amount of Selling Broker.

C. COUNTER OFFER: (_____)   (_____). By placing their initials here, Seller's acceptance is conditioned upon Buyer's accepting the attached counter offer in writing.

D. ACCEPTANCE: The undersigned Seller accepts the foregoing offer and agrees to sell the property described herein to the Buyer, and further acknowledges receipt of a copy hereof and authorizes Broker to deliver a signed copy to Buyer.

Date _____   Seller _____

Date _____   Seller _____

Date _____   Listing Office _____ By: _____

Address _____ Telephone _____

_____

Broker's Review _____   Date _____
               (Initials)

A REALTOR MAY ADVISE ON REAL ESTATE. IF YOU DESIRE LEGAL, TAX OR OTHER PROFESSIONAL ADVICE, CONSULT AN ATTORNEY, TAX ACCOUNTANT, GEOLOGIST OR OTHER PROFESSIONAL ADVISOR. THIS STANDARDIZED DOCUMENT IS FOR USE IN SIMPLE TRANSACTIONS. NO REPRESENTATION IS MADE REGARDING THE LEGAL VALIDITY OR ADEQUACY OF ANY PROVISION IN ANY SPECIFIC TRANSACTION. IT SHOULD NOT BE USED IN COMPLEX TRANSACTIONS OR WITH EXTENSIVE RIDERS OR ADDITIONS.

FINANCING ADDENDUM

(Seller Carryback)

This adendum is a part of the REAL ESTATE PURCHASE CONTRACT and RECEIPT for DEPOSIT, Dated

_____ _____ between _____ (Buyer)

and _____ (Seller) regarding

the real property described as _____

_____

_____

This contract is subject to and conditioned upon the Seller's written approval of Buyer's credit and financial

status within _____ calendar days from receipt of same.

Within five (5) calendar days of acceptance, Buyer shall provide Seller with customary financial statements for the sole purpose of approving credit and financial status of Buyer, by Seller, which approvall shall not be unreasonably withheld. Buyer authorizes Seller to engage the service of a credit reporting agency, at Buyer's expense, for credit approval process. Seller's failure to approve Buyer's credit and financial status shall render this contract null and void.

The following clauses shall apply and be incorporated in Note and/or Deed of Trust if initialed by Buyer and Seller:

    1. Seller (_____) (_____) Buyer (_____) (_____) Acceleration and/or Due on Sale Clause providing that, in the event of Buyer's Default or sale of the property or any interest therein, the Note(s) will, insofar as permitted by law, and at the Seller's option, become due and payable in full.

    2. Seller (_____) (_____) Buyer (_____) (_____) Request for notice of Default on all prior loans is to be recorded. The escrow agent is instructed to prepare, process, and record a request for notice in accordance with Civil Code.

    3. Seller (_____) (_____) Buyer (_____) (_____) Seller's acceptance is conditioned upon approval of Buyer's financial statement and credit report, within time limits as specified in the contract.

    4. Seller (_____) (_____) Buyer (_____) (_____) Late payment charge of six percent (6%) of the installment due or Five Dollars ($5.00), whichever is greater, if payment is received more than ten (10) days after the due date unless otherwise provided.

    5. Seller (_____) (_____) Buyer (_____) (_____) Fire and Extended Coverage Insurance shall be maintained by the Buyer in an amount equal to the total financing on the property, but not less than 80% of the replacement cost of the improvement, with the Seller named as loss payee.

    6. Seller (_____) (_____) Buyer (_____) (_____) Property Tax Service shall be obtained for the benefit of Seller, and paid by the Buyer.

    7. Seller (_____) (_____) Buyer (_____) (_____) Balloon Payment Provision: Buyer and Seller acknowledge that the financing provides for a single lump principal payment at maturity of said note. Buyer and Seller further acknowledge that they have not received or relied upon any statements or representations made to them by the Broker regarding availability of funds or rate of interest for which funds might be available when Buyer becomes obligated to refinance or pay off any loan payment pursuant to the terms of this agreement.

THE ARRANGER OF CREDIT IS RESPONSIBLE FOR FURNISHING FINANCIAL DISCLOSURE PER CIVIL CODE.

SELLER _____   BUYER _____

SELLER _____   BUYER _____

DATE _____   DATE _____

Contingency Removal Schedule

Date _____ Prepared by _____

Property Address: _____

Buyer: _____

Seller: _____

Date of Acceptance: _____ Escrow Company: _____

Estimated Close of Escrow: _____ Escrow Number: _____

CONTINGENCY	DAYS	DATE	STATUS
1. Financing Application	_____	_____	_____
2. Financing Pre-Qualifying	_____	_____	_____
3. Financing Contingency Removal	_____	_____	_____
4. Additional Deposit	_____	_____	_____
5. Preliminary Title Report			
A. Seller to Provide	_____	_____	_____
B. Buyer to Approve	_____	_____	_____
6. Structural Pest Control Report			
A. Seller to Provide	_____	_____	_____
B. Buyer to Approve	_____	_____	_____
7. Physical Inspection			
A. Buyer to Inspect	_____	_____	_____
B. Buyer to Approve	_____	_____	_____
8. Geological & Flood Hazard			
A. Seller to Provide	_____	_____	_____
B. Buyer to Approve	_____	_____	_____
9. Transfer Disclosure Statement			
A. Seller to Provide	_____	_____	_____
10. Other: _____	_____	_____	_____
_____	_____	_____	_____
_____	_____	_____	_____
_____	_____	_____	_____

CONTINGENCY RELEASE CLAUSE ADDENDUM

THIS IS INTENDED TO BE A LEGALLY BINDING CONTRACT. READ IT CAREFULLY.

CALIFORNIA ASSOCIATION OF REALTORS® (CAR) STANDARD FORM

This addendum is a part of the Real Estate Purchase Contract and Receipt for Deposit dated_____

Between _____ (Buyer)

and_____ (Seller)

regarding the real property described as_____

_____

Seller shall have the right to continue to offer subject property for sale.

Should a subsequent written offer be accepted by Seller, conditioned upon above named Buyer's Rights, Buyer

shall have _____ hours_____ days

following receipt of notice to remove and waive in writing the following condition(s) _____

_____

_____

_____

In the event Buyer(s) shall fail to remove the condition(s) within the above time limit, the Real Estate Purchase Contract and Receipt for Deposit and this agreement shall terminate and become null and void and Buyer's deposit shall be returned to Buyer.

Notice to Buyer to remove condition(s) shall be deemed to have been received by Buyer when Buyer, or his

agent, has received notice by delivery in person or by certified mail and addressed to _____

_____

If notice is given by mail Buyer shall have until 6:00 PM of the third day following the date of mailing, unless the notice provides otherwise, to deliver to Seller or Seller's agent Buyer's written agreement to remove and waive the contingencies.

The undersigned acknowledges receipt of a copy hereof.

RECEIPT IF DELIVERED IN PERSON

Receipt of this notice is acknowledged:

Dated _____   Buyer _____

                                                                               Buyer _____

Dated _____   Seller _____

                                                                               Seller _____

DISCLOSURE REGARDING
REAL ESTATE AGENCY RELATIONSHIPS
(As required by the Civil Code)
CALIFORNIA ASSOCIATION OF REALTORS® (CAR) STANDARD FORM

When you enter into a discussion with a real estate agent regarding a real estate transaction, you should from the outset understand what type of agency relationship or representation you wish to have with the agent in the transaction.

SELLER'S AGENT

A Seller's agent under a listing agreement with Seller acts as the agent for the Seller only. A Seller's agent or a subagent of that agent has the following affirmative obligations:

To the Seller:
(a) A Fiduciary duty of utmost care, integrity, honesty, and loyalty in dealings with the Seller.

To the Buyer & the Seller:
(a) Diligent exercise of reasonable skill and care in performance of the agent's duties.
(b) A duty of honest and fair dealing and good faith.
(c) A duty to disclose all facts known to the agent materially affecting the value or desirability of property that are not known to, or within the diligent attention and observation of, the parties.

An agent is not obligated to reveal to either party any confidential information obtained from the other party which does not involve the affirmative duties set forth above.

BUYER'S AGENT

A selling agent can, with a Buyer's consent, agree to act as agent for the Buyer only. In these situations, the agent is not the Seller's agent, even if by agreement the agent may receive compensation for services rendered, either in full or in part from the Seller. An agent acting only for a Buyer has the following affirmative obligations.

To the Buyer:
(a) A fiduciary duty of utmost care, integrity, honesty, and loyalty in dealings with the Buyer.

To the Buyer & Seller:
(a) Diligent exercise of reasonable skill and care in performance of the agent's duties.
(b) A duty of honest and fair dealing and good faith.
(c) A duty to disclose all facts known to the agent materially affecting the value or desirability of the property that are not known to, or within the diligent attention and observation of, the parties.

An agent is not obligated to reveal to either party any confidential information obtained from the other party which does not involve the affirmative duties set forth above.

AGENT REPRESENTING BOTH SELLER & BUYER

A real estate agent, either acting directly or through one or more associate licensees, can legally be the agent of both the Seller and the Buyer in a transaction, but only with the knowledge and consent of both the Seller and the Buyer.

In a dual agency situation, the agent has the following affirmative obligations to both the Seller and the Buyer:
(a) A fiduciary duty of utmost care, integrity, honesty and loyalty in the dealings with either Seller or the Buyer.
(b) Other duties to the Seller and the Buyer as stated above in their respective sections.

In representing both Seller and Buyer, the agent may not, without the express permission of the respective party, disclose to the other party that the Seller will accept a price less than the listing price or that the Buyer will pay a price greater than the price offered.

The above duties of the agent in a real estate transaction do not relieve a Seller or a Buyer from the responsibility to protect their own interests. You should carefully read all agreements to assure that they adequately express your understanding of the transaction. A real estate agent is a person qualified to advise about real estate. If legal or tax advice is desired, consult a competent professional.

Throughout your real property transaction you may receive more than one disclosure form, depending upon the number of agents assisting in the transaction. The law requires each agent with whom you have more than a casual relationship to present you with this disclosure form. You should read its contents each time it is presented to you, considering the relationship between you and the real estate agent in your specific transaction.

This disclosure form includes the provisions of article 2.5 (commencing with Section 2373) of Chapter 2 of Title 9 of Part 4 of Division 3 of the Civil Code set forth on the reverse hereof. Read it carefully.

I/WE ACKNOWLEDGE RECEIPT OF A COPY OF THIS DISCLOSURE.

BUYER/SELLER_____ Date_____ TIME_____ AM/PM

BUYER/SELLER_____ Date_____ TIME_____ AM/PM

AGENT _____ By_____ Date_____
(Please Print)   (Associate Licensee or Broker-Signature)

A REAL ESTATE BROKER IS QUALIFIED TO ADVISE ON REAL ESTATE. IF YOU DESIRE LEGAL ADVICE, CONSULT YOUR ATTORNEY.

This form is available for use by the entire real estate industry. The use of this form is not intended to identify the user as a REALTOR®. REALTOR® is a registered collective membership mark which may be used only by real estate licensees who are members of the NATIONAL ASSOCIATION OF REALTORS® and who subscribe to its Code of Ethics.

FORM AD-11

┌─ OFFICE USE ONLY ─┐
Reviewed by Broker or Designee _____
Date _____
└───────────────────┘

EQUAL HOUSING
OPPORTUNITY
SF-Feb-88

Comparative Market Analysis

Prepared for: _____

Prepared by: _____

Date: _____

RECENT SALES

Address	Br	Ba	Fr	Dr	Comments

Address	Br	Ba	Fr	Dr	Original List Price	Days on Mkt.	Price Sold	Date Sold	Comments

CURRENTLY LISTED

Address	Br	Ba	Fr	Dr	Original List Price	Days on Mkt.	Current List Price	Comments

Recommended price range

Marketing Plan

OBJECTIVE: To sell your property for highest price possible within a reasonable time with the least inconvenience to you.

Since more than two-thirds of residential real estate sales transactions are the result of a cooperative effort within the real estate brokerage community, it is extremely important to market your home to potential homebuyers **and** real estate agents in the market area. Fellowes Realty has developed the following marketing strategy in an effort to provide the greatest possible exposure of your property, both directly to the home buying public and indirectly through cooperating efforts with the real estate community:

1. Upon receipt of your signed listing, we will imput it into the appropriate MLS system as a first step toward full exposure to the entire real estate community.

2. A Fellowes Realty For Sale sign will be placed on the property .

3. I will council with you to be sure that we have properly prepared your home for showing and that you fully understand both of our roles in this process.

4. A computerized fact sheet will immediately be produced describing the most important features of your property for the benefit of prospective purchasers and other real estate agents interested in participating in the marketing of your property.

5. We will also order color brochures to be mailed to active agents in your market area, to immediate neighbors, and to our RELO affiliates for out-of town referrals. These brochures will also be available at every open house.

6. A Fellowes Realty office tour of your home will be arranged.

7. We will also arrange a broker's open house on tour day and provide each agent with a brochure and/or fact sheet detailing the home's features and amenities.

8. A lockbox will be placed on the property to ensure security, maximize ease for real estate agents attempting to show the house, and minimize inconvenience to you.

9. Advertising in the appropriate daily and weekly newspapers will be run on a regular and continuing basis until your home is sold.

Marketing Plan — Page 2

10. We will also advertise in Home & Land Magazine, which generates excellent responses from agents and the buying public alike.

11. Sunday open houses are a major marketing tool, and we recommend that your home be held open as often as possible. This activity ties in with newspaper advertising for maximum exposure.

12. I will keep track of potential buyers and follow up with other agents who have shown your home, and share with you any pertinent feedback that I am able to obtain. This information will be important in evaluating our marketing strategy and overcoming buyer's objections.

13. Our agents are continually calling upon major corporations and executive search firms involved in transferring people into the area. We are also a member of RELO, a major national referral organization.

14. Once an offer is submitted, I will advise you and help you obtain the best possible price and terms, as well as construct a clear and binding contract. You may wish to consult your accountant or tax attorney as well.

15. Finally, I will follow through on details that must be properly handled before a sale becomes final. These include the various inspections, loan papers, contingency removals, insurance, and escrow details.

PREPARING YOUR HOME FOR SALE

This is where you, the home owner, and I first become a team. WHEN I LIST YOUR HOME, WE WILL GO THROUGH IT TOGETHER, WORKING OUT A PLAN FOR PREPARING IT FOR SHOWING. Meanwhile, here are some of my tips for you to think about.

As your agent, I can determine value and provide maximum exposure, but in the final analysis, HOUSES SELL THEMSELVES.

SO LET YOUR HOME SMILE A WELCOME TO BUYERS.

PREPARING FOR SHOWING

1. IT ALL BEGINS WITH CURB APPEAL. Be sure your home makes the best possible first impression. The front door greets the prospect. Make sure it is fresh and clean. Dispose of any debris lying around. Hide garbage cans, bicycles, etc. Clean roof, gutters and downspouts. Scrape and repaint as necessary. Keep lawns trimmed and fertilized. Trim back shrubs, bushes, and low hanging tree branches that obstruct the view of the house. THEY WON'T BUY IT IF THEY CAN'T SEE IT!

2. GET READY TO MOVE - START PACKING. Very soon your house will be sold, so now is the perfect time to start packing. It's time to remove your "personality" from the house so that prospective buyers can picture themselves living there. First, dispose of everything you do not intend to take with you. Next, pack up little knick-knacks and items that might tend to clutter and make rooms look smaller. It may even be necessary to remove some furniture to make rooms appear larger. Make kitchen and bathroom counters appear as spacious as possible. Finally, display the full value of your garage, storage rooms, and other utility space by straightening up and removing all unnecessary items. Neat, well-ordered closets show that the space is ample.

3. REPAIRS THAT MAKE A DIFFERENCE. Minor repairs, such as fixing leaky faucets, loose door knobs, sticking doors and windows, warped cabinet drawers, faulty locks, and broken windows, should not be left undone. Cracks or holes in walls or ceilings detract tremendously, as does worn our carpeting or linoleum. Hardwood floors are considered a great asset. REFINISHING WILL PAY DIVIDENDS. Be sure all appliances are clean and in working order.

4. A LITTLE CLEANING GOES A LONG WAY. Now is the time for that spring house cleaning, even though it may not be spring. In addition to the normal cleaning, carpets should be shampooed and draperies dry cleaned.

PREPARING YOUR HOME FOR SALE - PAGE 2

5. LET THE SUN SHINE IN. Most prospects are immediately depressed by dark and dreary houses. Open draperies and curtains and let the prospect see how cheerful your home can be. Dark rooms simply do not appeal and seem smaller than they really are. Sometimes the addition of skylights is recommended to alleviate this problem. You may well receive more than the cost in return.

6. THE WONDERS OF FRESH PAINT. Faded walls and worn woodwork reduce appeal, and most prospects cannot visualize beyond what they see. Paint as required. The colors should be light and neutral. Preferably off-white or pale earth tones. Installing wallpaper should be discouraged. Remember, your tastes will rarely be the same as that of the next owner.

SHOWING THE HOUSE

1. LET ME EARN MY KEEP. I have been highly trained to deal with your prospective buyers or their agents. By acting on your behalf, I can protect your interests in many ways that will become ever more apparent as our relationship grows, providing you allow me, and me alone, to conduct the business of selling your home. Never discuss price, terms, or any other business matters with prospects or their agents. Simply put: YOU MAKE THE DECISIONS & I DO THE TALKING.

2. THREE'S A CROWD. Prospective buyers are most relaxed in viewing homes when the owners are not present. They will **not** voice objections in the presence of the owner, making it impossible for the agent to overcome any such objections. It is also very difficult for the prospects to visualize themselves living in the home when the owners are deeply entrenched in their own lifestyle during the showing.

3. SILENCE IS GOLDEN. Be courteous but don't force conversation with prospective buyers. They are there to inspect the house, not to pay a social call. Even though you suspect they might miss important features in your house, always let the agents do the showing. It is my responsibility to point out these features in a well prepared fact sheet which will always be available for agents or prospects viewing the home.

4. CREATE A WARM, INVITING AMBIENCE. Turn on lights in strategic areas, even during the day. At night, turn them all on. Have the stereo FM playing quiet classical or "easy listening" music for all showings. The aroma of a simmering brew of potpourri or cinnamon and cider will greatly enhance the appeal.

TEAMWORK FOR SUCCESS

I am committed to selling your home at the highest possible price in the shortest possible time. I am relying upon you to provide the most appealing product possible. WORKING TOGETHER, WE MAKE A GREAT TEAM!.

MENLO PARK - ATHERTON BOARD OF REALTORS
MULTIPLE LISTING SERVICE
A Participant in the Regional Data Service
Confidential Information

For the use of M.L.S. participants only. This material is copyrighted and the copyright is reserved to the publisher. Unauthorized duplication of this material will be considered a violation of copyright and subject to legal action.

THIS IS INTENDED TO BE A LEGALLY BINDING AGREEMENT — READ IT CAREFULLY

1. EMPLOYMENT. For and in consideration of the services to be performed by_____
a licensed Real Estate Broker, hereinafter called Agent, I (property owner) hereby employ said Agent as my sole and exclusive Agent to sell the following described property commonly known as_____
_____and grant said Agent Exclusive Right to Sell said property and accept a deposit thereon for the price of_____on the following terms_____

2. TERM. Agent's right to sell shall begin on_____19___and expire at midnight on_____19___. Agent is authorized to submit this listing to the Menlo Park-Atherton Board of Realtors Multiple Listing Service, a participant in the Regional Data Service, for publication. Upon close of escrow Agent is authorized to report the sale price and other pertinent information for the information, publication, dissemination and use of the authorized users of the Multiple Listing Service. Seller and Agent agree that the information contained herein is confidential and shall be made available only to the authorized users of the Multiple Listing Service.

3. BROKERAGE FEE. NOTE: THE AMOUNT OR RATE OF REAL ESTATE COMMISSIONS IS NOT FIXED BY LAW. THEY ARE SET BY EACH BROKER INDIVIDUALLY AND MAY BE NEGOTIABLE BETWEEN THE SELLER AND THE BROKER.

Seller agrees to pay Agent a brokerage fee of_____if, during the term of this listing the property is sold or exchanged by said Agent, or by seller, or by any other Agent, or if said property be withdrawn from sale, transferred, or leased without approval of said Agent, or if performance hereunder by Agent is prevented by Seller. Brokerage fee will be deemed to have been earned when the Agent, or anyone else procures a buyer who is "ready, willing, and able" to purchase the property on the listing terms or any other terms acceptable to the seller.

4. BROKERAGE FEE ON BUYER DEFAULT. If a deposit is retained, one half of same shall be retained by or paid to Agent and one half to Seller provided, however, that said Agent's portion of any such deposit shall not exceed the amount of the aforesaid compensation.

5. SALE/TRANSFER AFTER EXPIRATION. Seller further agrees to pay the compensation provided for above, if the property is sold, conveyed, or otherwise transferred within_____days after the termination of this authority or any extension thereof to anyone with whom Agent has had negotiations prior to final termination, provided Seller has received notice in writing, including the names of the prospective purchasers, before or upon termination of this agreement or any extension thereof. However, Seller shall not be obligated to pay the compensation provided for in this paragraph if a valid listing agreement is subsequently entered into during the term of said protection period with another licensed real estate broker, and a sale, lease or exchange of the property is made during the term of said protection.

6. CONDITION OF PREMISES. Seller agrees not to rent, lease or change the terms of any existing rental or lease without notifying the Agent. Seller agrees to show said property at reasonable hours. Seller agrees to maintain property in at least its present condition during the term of this agreement or until close of escrow or transfer of possession, whichever first occurs. Seller agrees that heating, plumbing, electrical, sewer/septic systems, appliances, and/or equipment are in good working order except as herein noted._____

7. TITLE, ESCROW, PRORATIONS. Evidence of good merchantable title to be in the form of deed and policy of title insurance by a responsible title company, to be furnished and paid for by_____. The charge for escrow service to be paid by_____. Where applicable interest, taxes, rent and Home Owner's Association dues are to be prorated. Assessments for improvements now in construction or recently completed or now a lien are to be paid by_____or prorated_____.

8. TRANSFER TAXES. County real property transfer tax to be paid by_____. Any city transfer tax, where required, to be paid by_____.

9. DISCLOSURES.

		(Initial below)	YES	NO
a)	Offer of Sub-Agency			
b)	Seller authorizes Agent to place a FOR SALE SIGN on property.			
c)	Seller authorizes Agent to place a LOCK BOX on property.			
d)	Seller has been advised of various home protection plans available.			
e)	Is Sellers property in a Special Study Zone?			
f)	Is Sellers property in a Flood Control Zone?			
g)	Will Seller provide Geological/Flood Determination Report?			
h)	Seller to provide current Structural Pest Control report.			
i)	Seller to provide any community data report as required.			
j)	Foreign Investment in Real Property Tax Act (FIRPTA) disclosure required (see reverse).			

10. BUILDING PERMITS. Seller represents that he has made no additions or alterations to the property nor does he have any knowledge of any additions or alterations being made to the property without appropriate building permits and inspections, except as herein noted:_____

11. INDEMNIFICATION. Seller agrees to indemnify and hold Agent safe and harmless from any liability or damages arising from any incorrect or incomplete information supplied by Seller to said Agent. Seller further agrees that the agent is not responsible for vandalism, theft, or damage of any nature whatsoever to the property or its contents.

12. ATTORNEY'S FEES. If any party to this agreement shall institute any legal action against any other party to this agreement, the prevailing party shall be entitled to court costs and reasonable attorney's fees in addition to any other judgment of the court.

13. DISCRIMINATION. This property is offered without respect to race, creed, color, sex, or national origin.

14. AGENCY. By placing his initials here (_____) (_____) the Seller(s) consents to the listing agent also acting as the agent for the Buyer.

I HAVE READ THE FOREGOING CONTRACT AND AGREE TO ALL OF ITS TERMS AND CONDITIONS AND ACKNOWLEDGE RECEIPT OF A COPY THEREOF ON——————————————————————————19———.

SELLER——————————————————————SELLER————————————————————————

Address——————————————————————City——————————State——————————Zip————————

*Signature of all owners required. Indicate if sole owner.

In consideration of the above employment, the undersigned Agent agrees to use due diligence in procuring a purchaser.

LISTING BROKER————————————————————————————————DATE————————————

LISTING SALESPERSON————————————————————————————DATE————————————

No Representation is made as to the legal validity of any provision or the adequacy of any provision in any specific transaction.
A Real Estate Broker is the person qualified to advise on Real Estate. If you desire legal advice consult your attorney.

Rev. 7-87

SINGLE FAMILY RESIDENTIAL
CLASS 1

REALTOR   EQUAL HOUSING OPPORTUNITY   1 SFR

KEYWORDS: Fill in the boxes for each Keyword. Enter information as prompted by the computer. (R)'s denote required entries for adding a listing.

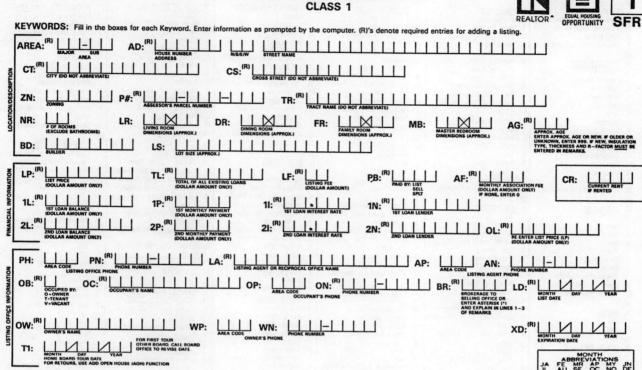

LOCATION/DESCRIPTION

AREA: (R)   MAJOR SUB AREA   AD: (R) HOUSE NUMBER ADDRESS   N/S/E/W   STREET NAME

CT: (R) CITY (DO NOT ABBREVIATE)   CS: (R) CROSS STREET (DO NOT ABBREVIATE)

ZN: ZONING   P#: (R) ASSESSOR'S PARCEL NUMBER   TR: (R) TRACT NAME (DO NOT ABBREVIATE)

NR: # OF ROOMS (EXCLUDE BATHROOMS)   LR: LIVING ROOM DIMENSIONS (APPROX.)   DR: DINING ROOM DIMENSIONS (APPROX.)   FR: FAMILY ROOM DIMENSIONS (APPROX.)   MB: MASTER BEDROOM DIMENSIONS (APPROX.)   AG: (R) APPROX. AGE ENTER APPROX. AGE OR NEW. IF OLDER OR UNKNOWN, ENTER 999. IF NEW, INSULATION TYPE, THICKNESS AND R–FACTOR MUST BE ENTERED IN REMARKS.

BD: BUILDER   LS: LOT SIZE (APPROX.)

FINANCIAL INFORMATION

LP: (R) LIST PRICE (DOLLAR AMOUNT ONLY)   TL: TOTAL OF ALL EXISTING LOANS (DOLLAR AMOUNT ONLY)   LF: LISTING FEE (DOLLAR AMOUNT)   PB: (R) PAID BY: LIST SELL SPLT   AF: (R) MONTHLY ASSOCIATION FEE (DOLLAR AMOUNT ONLY) IF NONE, ENTER 0   CR: CURRENT RENT IF RENTED

1L: (R) 1ST LOAN BALANCE (DOLLAR AMOUNT ONLY)   1P: (R) 1ST MONTHLY PAYMENT (DOLLAR AMOUNT ONLY)   1I: 1ST LOAN INTEREST RATE   1N: (R) 1ST LOAN LENDER

2L: (R) 2ND LOAN BALANCE (DOLLAR AMOUNT ONLY)   2P: (R) 2ND MONTHLY PAYMENT (DOLLAR AMOUNT ONLY)   2I: 2ND LOAN INTEREST RATE   2N: (R) 2ND LOAN LENDER   OL: (R) RE-ENTER LIST PRICE (LP) (DOLLAR AMOUNT ONLY)

LISTING OFFICE INFORMATION

PH: AREA CODE   PN: (R) LISTING OFFICE PHONE   PHONE NUMBER   LA: (R) LISTING AGENT OR RECIPROCAL OFFICE NAME   AP: AREA CODE   AN: LISTING AGENT PHONE   PHONE NUMBER

OB: (R) OCCUPIED BY: O = OWNER T = TENANT V = VACANT   OC: (R) OCCUPANT'S NAME   OP: AREA CODE   ON: (R) OCCUPANT'S PHONE   PHONE NUMBER   BR: (R) BROKERAGE TO SELLING OFFICE OR ENTER ASTERISK (*) AND EXPLAIN IN LINES 1–3 OF REMARKS   LD: (R) MONTH DAY YEAR LIST DATE

OW: (R) OWNER'S NAME   WP: AREA CODE   WN: OWNER'S PHONE   PHONE NUMBER   XD: (R) MONTH DAY YEAR EXPIRATION DATE

T1: MONTH DAY YEAR HOME BOARD TOUR DATE FOR RETOURS, USE ADD OPEN HOUSE (AOH) FUNCTION   FOR FIRST TOUR OTHER BOARD, CALL BOARD OFFICE TO REVISE DATE.

MONTH ABBREVIATIONS
JA FE MR AP MY JN
JL AU SE OC NO DE

FEATURES: For Adding a Listing, underline the appropriate Feature selection(s). Features with an (R) must have at least one selection underlined.

COPYRIGHT 1987, NORTH SAN MATEO COUNTY—SAN MATEO-BURLINGAME—REDWOOD CITY-SAN CARLOS-BELMONT—PACIFICA-HALF MOON BAY MULTIPLE LISTING SERVICE

(R)
A. TYPE
1. Detached Single Family House
2. Attached Single Family House
3. Tract House
4. Other—Specify in Remarks

(R)
B. STYLE/STORIES
1. Ranch
2. Elevated Ranch
3. Two Story
4. Split Level
5. Tri Level
6. Tudor
7. Spanish
8. French
9. Eichler
10. Colonial
11. Contemporary
12. Cape Cod
13. Victorian
14. Georgian
15. Other—Specify in Remarks

(R)
C. BEDROOMS
1. One
2. Two
3. Three
4. Four
5. Five
6. Six or More
7. Studio
8. Ground Floor Bedroom
9. Master Bedroom Suite
10. Two or More Master Suites

(R)
D. BATHS
1. One
2. Two
3. Three
4. Four or More
5. One + 1/2
6. Two + 1/2
7. Three + 1/2
8. More Than One 1/2 Bath
9. Septic System
10. Other—Specify in Remarks

E. SHOWER/TUB
1. Stall Shower
2. 2 or More Stall Showers
3. Shower Over Tub
4. 2 or More Showers Over Tub
5. Tub
6. Two or More Tubs
7. Bidet
8. Sunken Tub
9. Tub With Jets
10. Other—Specify in Remarks

(R)
F. DINING AREA
1. Separate Dining Room
2. Family Kitchen
3. Eat-in Kitchen
4. LR/DR Combo
5. Breakfast Room
6. Breakfast Bar
7. Other—Specify in Remarks

G. FIREPLACE
1. Freestanding
2. Wood Burning
3. Gas Log Only
4. Gas Starter
5. Wood Stove
6. Fireplace Insert
7. In Living Room
8. In Family Room
9. In Master Bedroom
10. Two or More Fireplaces
11. Other—Specify in Remarks

H. FLOORS
1. Wall-to-Wall Carpet
2. Partial Hardwood
3. Hardwood
4. Linoleum/Vinyl
5. Tile
6. Marble
7. Slab
8. Wood
9. Other—Specify in Remarks

(R)
I. HEATING/COOLING
1. Gas
2. Electric
3. Bottled Gas
4. Central Forced Air
5. Wall Furnace
6. Floor Furnace
7. Radiant
8. Baseboard
9. Steam/Hot Water
10. Heat Pump
11. Solar
12. Central Air Conditioning
13. Some Room Air Conditioner(s)
14. NONE
15. Other—Specify in Remarks

J. ROOF
1. Tile
2. Slate
3. Concrete
4. Metal
5. Rock
6. Wood
7. Composition
8. Shingle
9. Shake
10. Tar & Gravel
11. Other—Specify in Remarks

K. EXTERIOR SIDING
1. Stucco
2. Brick
3. Shingle
4. Wood
5. Stone
6. Metal
7. Other Siding
8. Shared/Common Wall
9. Other—Specify in Remarks

(R)
L. GARAGE/PARKING
1. 1 Car Garage
2. 2 Car Garage
3. 3 or More Car Garage
4. 1 Car Carport
5. 2 or More Car Carport
6. Detached
7. RV/Boat Parking
8. Guest Parking Area
9. Off-Street Parking
10. Garage-Converted
11. Underground Parking
12. Electronic Door Opener
13. Street Parking Only
14. Other—Specify in Remarks

M. LOT DESCRIPTION
1. Waterfront
2. View
3. Cul de sac
4. Corner
5. Leased Land
6. Level
7. Sloped Up (from Street)
8. Sloped Down (from Street)
9. Landscaped
10. Possible Tennis Site
11. Possible Pool Site
12. 1/2 to 1 Acre
13. 1+ to 5 Acres
14. 5 + Acres
15. Other—Specify in Remarks

(R)
N. YARDS/GROUNDS
1. Guest House
2. Horse(s) Permitted
3. Tennis Court
4. Sport Court
5. Boat Dock
6. Deck
7. Patio
8. Well
9. Patio/Deck Covered/Enclosed
10. Fenced Yard
11. Sprinklers—Front
12. Sprinklers—Rear
13. Automatic Sprinkler(s)
14. Barbecue Area
15. Other—Specify in Remarks

O. SPA/POOL
1. Spa
2. Hot Tub
3. Pool/Spa Combo
4. Pool-In Ground
5. Pool-Above Ground
6. Heater
7. No Heater
8. Solar
9. Black Bottom
10. Lap Only
11. Association Pool and/or Spa
12. Membership Fee
13. Pool Sweep Included
14. Maintenance Equipment Included
15. Other—Specify in Remarks

P. EXISTING FINANCING
1. Clear
2. VA/FHA
3. CAL-VET
4. Private
5. 1st Loan—Fixed
6. 1st Loan-Variable/Adjustable
7. 1st. Loan—Convertible
8. 2nd Loan-Fixed
9. 2nd Loan-Variable/Adjustable
10. 1st Loan-PI
11. 1st Loan-Interest Only
12. 2nd Loan-Interest Only
13. Impounds Included
14. Balloon Payment(s)
15. Other—Specify in Remarks

(R)
Q. NEW TERMS
1. All Cash
2. Conventional
3. Owner May Carry 1st
4. Owner May Carry 2nd/Other
5. Assumable Financing Available
6. Assumption Restricted
7. PrePay Penalty (Use Existing Lender)
8. VA Possible
9. FHA Possible
10. Lease Option
11. Trade
12. Tax Exchange
13. Submit
14. Other—Specify in Remarks

(R)
R. OTHER ROOMS
1. Family Room
2. Den/Study
3. Laundry Room
4. Laundry Area
5. Library
6. Extra Storage
7. Recreation/Bonus Room
8. Workshop
9. Formal Entry
10. Separate Apartment
11. Full Basement
12. Partial Basement
13. Attic
14. Maid's Quarters
15. Solarium

S. PRICE INCLUDES
1. Refrigerator
2. Range/Oven
3. Self-Cleaning Oven
4. 2 or More Ovens
5. Dishwasher
6. Disposal
7. Window Coverings
8. Tacked Down Carpet
9. Trash Compactor
10. Washer
11. Dryer
12. Microwave Oven
13. Water Treatment System
14. Fire Sprinklers
15. Central Fire Alarm System

T. MISCELLANEOUS
1. 220 Volts
2. Water Well
3. Gas Hookup
4. Elevator
5. Satellite Dish
6. Sauna
7. Atrium
8. Greenhouse
9. Wet Bar
10. Security Features
11. Air Purifier Built In
12. Handicapped Features
13. Built-in Vacuum
14. Cable TV Available
15. Intercom

(R)
U. ENERGY AUDIT
1. Weather Stripped Doors
2. Insulated Hot Water Heater
3. Low-Flow Shower Head(s)
4. Caulked & Sealed Openings
5. Insulated Heating and Cooling Ducts
6. Energy Other—Specify in Remarks
7. City-County Audit Required

HOMEOWNERS PROTECTION PLAN
9. Provided
10. Split 50/50

(R)
V. SPECIAL INFORMATION
1. Special Study Zone-YES
2. Special Study Zone-NO
3. Flood Area-YES (Flood Insurance Required)
4. Flood Area-NO
5. Sewer/Septic Inspection Required
6. Smoke Detector(s) are Installed
7. Smoke Detector(s) need to be Installed
8. Bonds/Assessments
9. Leased Land
10. Agent Has Not Inspected Property
11. Call Listing Agent Before Writing Deposit Receipt
12. Seller is Licensed Real Estate Agent
13. Agent is Related to Seller
14. Buyer's Financial Statement Required
15. Other—Specify in Remarks

(R)
W. DOCUMENTS AVAILABLE
1. Real Estate Transfer Disclosure Statement
2. Pest Control Report
3. Property Inspection Report(s)
4. Roof Report
5. Pool Report
6. Association Documents
7. Land Lease
8. Bond/Assessments
9. Sewer/Septic Report
10. Water Test(s) Logs
11. Rental/Lease Agreements
12. NONE
13. Other—Specify in Remarks

X. TYPE OF LISTING
1. Exclusive Right to Sell (ER)
2. Exclusive Agency (EA)
3. Non-Exclusive Agency (NE)

PROBATE/CONSERVATORSHIP
4. Court Confirmation Required (CC)
5. No Court Confirmation Required (NC)
6. Other—Specify in Remarks

U.S. FEDERAL TAXPAYER (FIRPTA)
7. YES
8. NO

COOPERATING BROKER AGENT FOR:
9. Seller
10. Buyer
11. Buyer & Seller
12. Any of the Above

(R)
Y. CITY TRANSFER TAX
1. Split 50/50
2. Seller Pays
3. Buyer Pays
4. NONE

(R) PRINTING INSTRUCTIONS
5. Photo Requested
6. No Photo
7. Photo/Map/Rendering Submitted

(R)
Z. SHOWING INSTRUCTIONS
1. District 25 Keybox
2. RDS Keysafe
3. Other Keybox-CALL
4. Key in Listing Office
5. Call First—Keybox
6. Appointment Only
7. Vacant
8. Call Listing Agent
9. Call Occupant
10. Tenant Occupied
11. Advance Notice Required
12. Locked Main Entrance Gate (See Remarks)
13. SPECIAL INSTRUCTIONS- Call Listing Agent
14. Make Offer—Subject to Inspection
15. Other—Specify in Remarks

FOR BROKER'S USE ONLY

FOR REMARKS, CONTINUE TO PAGE 2

COMPANY NAME _____

BY: _____
AGENT'S SIGNATURE _____ DATE _____

READ & APPROVED BY: _____

OWNER'S SIGNATURE _____ DATE _____

OWNER'S SIGNATURE _____ DATE _____

ENTER MLS NUMBER ASSIGNED BY COMPUTER

OFFICE BROKER CODE

OFFICE   BRANCH

MULTIPLE LISTING SERVICE

REMARKS FORM

CLASS (R) ☐☐ (1-11)

LP: (R) ☐☐☐☐☐☐☐ LIST PRICE

AREA: (R) ☐☐☐—☐☐ MAJOR | SUB | AREA

AD: (R) _____
ADDRESS OF PROPERTY

CT: (R) _____
CITY

LA: (R) _____
LISTING AGENT NAME

REMARKS: Enter up to 304 characters (including spaces and punctuation) for new construction insulation factors or any other information about the listing. Lines 1, 2 and 3 will appear in the book.

LINE 1: ☐☐☐☐☐☐☐☐☐☐☐☐☐☐☐☐☐☐☐☐☐☐☐☐☐☐☐☐☐☐☐☐☐☐☐☐☐☐
☐☐☐☐☐☐☐☐☐☐☐☐☐☐☐☐☐☐☐☐☐☐☐☐☐☐☐☐☐☐☐☐☐☐☐☐☐☐

LINE 2: ☐☐☐☐☐☐☐☐☐☐☐☐☐☐☐☐☐☐☐☐☐☐☐☐☐☐☐☐☐☐☐☐☐☐☐☐☐☐
☐☐☐☐☐☐☐☐☐☐☐☐☐☐☐☐☐☐☐☐☐☐☐☐☐☐☐☐☐☐☐☐☐☐☐☐☐☐

LINE 3: ☐☐☐☐☐☐☐☐☐☐☐☐☐☐☐☐☐☐☐☐☐☐☐☐☐☐☐☐☐☐☐☐☐☐☐☐☐☐
☐☐☐☐☐☐☐☐☐☐☐☐☐☐☐☐☐☐☐☐☐☐☐☐☐☐☐☐☐☐☐☐☐☐☐☐☐☐

LINE 4: ☐☐☐☐☐☐☐☐☐☐☐☐☐☐☐☐☐☐☐☐☐☐☐☐☐☐☐☐☐☐☐☐☐☐☐☐☐☐
☐☐☐☐☐☐☐☐☐☐☐☐☐☐☐☐☐☐☐☐☐☐☐☐☐☐☐☐☐☐☐☐☐☐☐☐☐☐

BOXED AREA WILL NOT APPEAR IN THE BOOK.

ADDITIONAL REMARKS: Enter up to 152 characters (including spaces and punctuation) to continue remarks or detail directions to the property.

LINE 1: ☐☐☐☐☐☐☐☐☐☐☐☐☐☐☐☐☐☐☐☐☐☐☐☐☐☐☐☐☐☐☐☐☐☐☐☐☐☐
☐☐☐☐☐☐☐☐☐☐☐☐☐☐☐☐☐☐☐☐☐☐☐☐☐☐☐☐☐☐☐☐☐☐☐☐☐☐

LINE 2: ☐☐☐☐☐☐☐☐☐☐☐☐☐☐☐☐☐☐☐☐☐☐☐☐☐☐☐☐☐☐☐☐☐☐☐☐☐☐
☐☐☐☐☐☐☐☐☐☐☐☐☐☐☐☐☐☐☐☐☐☐☐☐☐☐☐☐☐☐☐☐☐☐☐☐☐☐

COMPANY NAME _____

OWNER'S SIGNATURE _____ DATE _____

BY: _____
AGENT'S SIGNATURE _____ DATE _____

OWNER'S SIGNATURE _____ DATE _____

FOR BROKER'S USE ONLY

ENTER MLS NUMBER ASSIGNED BY COMPUTER
☐☐☐☐☐☐☐☐

OFFICE BROKER CODE
☐☐☐☐☐☐
OFFICE | BRANCH

SELLER'S AFFIDAVIT
OF NONFOREIGN STATUS
CALIFORNIA ASSOCIATION OF REALTORS® (CAR) STANDARD FORM
(FOREIGN INVESTMENT IN REAL PROPERTY TAX ACT)

Section 1445 of the Internal Revenue Code provides that a transferee of a U.S. real property interest must withhold tax if the transferor is a foreign person. Sections 18805(a)(2) and 26131(a)(2) of the California Revenue and Taxation Code provide that a transferee of a California real property interest must withhold tax if the transferor is a foreign person. To inform the transferee that withholding of tax is not required upon the disposition of a U.S. and/or California real property interest located at _____

by _____ [name of transferor(s)].
I hereby certify the following (if an entity transferor, on behalf of the transferor):

THIS SECTION FOR INDIVIDUAL TRANSFEROR [NUMBER 1]:

1. I am not a nonresident alien for purposes of U.S. income taxation;

2. My U.S. taxpayer identification number (Social Security number) is _____ ;and

3. My home address is_____

THIS SECTION FOR INDIVIDUAL TRANSFEROR [NUMBER 2]:

1. I am not a nonresident alien for purposes of U.S. income taxation;

2. My U.S. taxpayer identification number (Social Security number) is _____ ;and

3. My home address is_____

THIS SECTION FOR CORPORATION, PARTNERSHIP, TRUST, OR ESTATE TRANSFEROR [NUMBER 3]:

1. _____ [name of transferor]
   is not a foreign corporation, foreign partnership, foreign trust, or foreign estate (as those terms are defined in the Internal Revenue Code and Income Tax Regulations);

2. _____ [name of transferor]'s U.S. employer
   identification number is _____ ;

3. _____[name of transferor]'s office address
   is _____ ; and

4. I, the undersigned individual, declare that I have authority to sign this document on behalf of
   _____ [name of transferor]

THIS SECTION FOR ALL TRANSFEROR(S):

_____ [name of transferor]
understands that this certification may be disclosed to the Internal Revenue Service and to the California Franchise Tax Board by transferee and that any false statement I have made herein (or for entity transferor, contained herein) could be punished by fine, imprisonment, or both.

Under penalties of perjury I declare that I have examined this certification and to the best of my knowledge and belief it is true, correct and complete.

Date _____ Signature [Number 1] _____

Typed or Printed Name _____

Date _____ Signature [Number 2] _____

Typed or Printed Name _____

Date _____ Signature [Number 3] _____

Typed or Printed Name _____

Title [if signed on behalf
of an entity transferor] _____

IMPORTANT NOTICE: An affidavit should be signed by each individual or entity transferor to whom or to which it applies. Before you sign, any questions relating to the legal sufficiency of this form, or to whether it applies to a particular transaction, or to the definition of any of the terms used, should be referred to an attorney, certified public accountant, other professional tax advisor, the Internal Revenue Service, or the California Franchise Tax Board.

This form is available for use by the entire real estate industry. The use of this form is not intended to identify the user as a REALTOR®. REALTOR® is a registered collective membership mark which may be used only by real estate licensees who are members of the NATIONAL ASSOCIATION OF REALTORS® and who subscribe to its Code of Ethics.

┌─────────────────────────────────────┐
│ ── OFFICE USE ONLY ──   │
│ Reviewed by Broker or Designee _____ │
│   Date _____   │
└─────────────────────────────────────┘

Copyright© 1988, CALIFORNIA ASSOCIATION OF REALTORS®
525 South Virgil Avenue, Los Angeles, California 90020   FORM AS-14

EQUAL HOUSING
OPPORTUNITY
SF-Dec-88

Checklist for Presentation of Offers

Check Complete

I use this checklist to protect your interests when offers are presented on your property:

1. Terms are clear and complete. ☐

2. Loan Information
   A. Is the anticipated loan **realistic?** ☐
   B. Is there an interest rate - not to exceed _____ %? ☐
   C. Is the buyer to go back through the existing lender? ☐
   D. Prequalifying letter to be removed in writing. ☐
   E. Number of days to qualify for and obtain the new loan. ☐
   F. Loan contingency to be removed in writing. ☐

3. **IMPORTANT** - Additional deposit to be increased upon removal of loan contingency. ☐

4. If Seller is to carry first loan:
   A. Insurance coverage - naming beneficiary as insured on fire policy. ☐
   B. Financial statement and credit report from the buyer. ☐
   C. Is down payment sufficient to create secure loan/value ratio? ☐
   D. Interest rate. ☐
   E. Term - All due and payable in _____ years. ☐
   F. Payable $ _____ monthly. ☐
   G. Acceleration clause - due on sale clause. ☐
   H. Tax service. ☐

5. Seller to carry second loan:
   A. All of number 4, above, plus: ☐
   B. Payment greater than 1% of face value. ☐
   C. Request for notice of default on first trust deed. ☐

6. Date of closing. ☐

7. Date of occupancy - provision made for rental, if possession not upon close of escrow. ☐

8. Any variation in payment of normal closing costs for buyer and seller.
   A. Transfer tax: Who pays? ☐
   B. Title Insurance: Who pays? ☐
   C. Escrow Fee: Who pays? ☐

10. Is structural pest control certification agreement completed with limitation for expenditures by seller, if required? ☐

(continued)

Checklist for Presentation of Offers — Page 2

Check Complete

11. Inspections:
    A. Who pays? ☐
    B. Time limit. ☐

12. What repairs, if any, are to be made; by whom and with what dollar limitation, if any? ☐

13. Have you made written disclosure of any deficiency, within or affecting the property
    or structure which might adversely affect the value, use or enjoyment of the property or
    structure by buyer? **(Required by law, effective 7-1-85)** ☐
    A. Additions or alterations - with or without permits. ☐
    B. Building code considerations. ☐

14. Are all the necessary addenda checked?
    A. Flood Control Act ☐
    B. Special studies ☐
    C. Structural pest control. ☐
    D. FHA/VA. ☐
    E. Occupancy agreements. ☐
    F. FIRPTA. ☐
    G. Agency disclosure. ☐

15. Liquidated damages clause - initialed or signed by buyer and seller, if requested. ☐

16. Signatures by all buyers named in the contract. ☐

17. Bonds or assessments - paid by seller, assumed by buyer, or prorated. ☐

18. Sale of buyer's home.
    A. Contingency release clause - 72 hour release clause. ☐
    B. Verify that the number of days to sell corresponds with the close of escrow. ☐

19. If broker is acting as principal, then disclosure is required. ☐

20. Do buyers and sellers completely understand costs to be incurred, payments to be made
    and estimated net revenue to be realized from this transaction. ☐

REAL ESTATE TRANSFER DISCLOSURE STATEMENT
(CALIFORNIA CIVIL CODE 1102, ET SEQ.)
CALIFORNIA ASSOCIATION OF REALTORS® (CAR) STANDARD FORM

THIS DISCLOSURE STATEMENT CONCERNS THE REAL PROPERTY SITUATED IN THE CITY OF _____
_____, **COUNTY OF**_____ , **STATE OF CALIFORNIA**
DESCRIBED AS _____ .
THIS STATEMENT IS A DISCLOSURE OF THE CONDITION OF THE ABOVE DESCRIBED PROPERTY IN COMPLIANCE WITH SECTION 1102 OF THE CIVIL CODE AS OF _____ , **19**_____ . **IT IS NOT A WARRANTY OF ANY KIND BY THE SELLER(S) OR ANY AGENT(S) REPRESENTING ANY PRINCIPAL(S) IN THIS TRANSACTION, AND IS NOT A SUBSTITUTE FOR ANY INSPECTIONS OR WARRANTIES THE PRINCIPAL(S) MAY WISH TO OBTAIN.**

I
COORDINATION WITH OTHER DISCLOSURE FORMS

This Real Estate Transfer Disclosure Statement is made pursuant to Section 1102 of the Civil Code. Other statutes require disclosures, depending upon the details of the particular real estate transaction (for example: special study zone and purchase—money liens on residential property).

Substituted Disclosures: The following disclosures have or will be made in connection with this real estate transfer, and are intended to satisfy the disclosure obligations on this form, where the subject matter is the same: _____
_____
_____
_____

(list all substituted disclosure forms to be used in connection with this transaction)

II
SELLER'S INFORMATION

The Seller discloses the following information with the knowledge that even though this is not a warranty, prospective Buyers may rely on this information in deciding whether and on what terms to purchase the subject property. Seller hereby authorizes any agent(s) representing any principal(s) in this transaction to provide a copy of this statement to any person or entity in connection with any actual or anticipated sale of the property.

THE FOLLOWING ARE REPRESENTATIONS MADE BY THE SELLER(S) AND ARE NOT THE REPRESENTATIONS OF THE AGENT(S), IF ANY. THIS INFORMATION IS A DISCLOSURE AND IS NOT INTENDED TO BE PART OF ANY CONTRACT BETWEEN THE BUYER AND SELLER.

Seller ☐ is ☐ is not occupying the property.

A. The subject property has the items checked below (read across):

☐ Range	☐ Oven	☐ Microwave
☐ Dishwasher	☐ Trash Compactor	☐ Garbage Disposal
☐ Washer/Dryer Hookups	☐ Window Screens	☐ Rain Gutters
☐ Burglar Alarms	☐ Smoke Detector(s)	☐ Fire Alarm
☐ T.V. Antenna	☐ Satellite Dish	☐ Intercom
☐ Central Heating	☐ Central Air Conditioning	☐ Evaporator Cooler(s)
☐ Wall/Window Air Conditioning	☐ Sprinklers	☐ Public Sewer System
☐ Septic Tank	☐ Sump Pump	☐ Water Softener
☐ Patio/Decking	☐ Built-in Barbeque	☐ Gazebo
☐ Sauna	☐ Pool	☐ Spa ☐ Hot Tub
☐ Security Gate(s)	☐ Garage Door Opener(s)	☐ Number of Remote Controls _____
Garage: ☐ Attached	☐ Not Attached	☐ Carport
Pool/Spa Heater: ☐ Gas	☐ Solar	☐ Electric
Water Heater: ☐ Gas	☐ Solar	☐ Electric
Water Supply: ☐ City	☐ Well	☐ Private Utility ☐ Other _____
Gas Supply: ☐ Utility	☐ Bottled	

Exhaust Fan(s) in _____ 220 Volt Wiring in_____
Fireplace(s) in _____ ☐ Gas Starter
☐ Roof(s): Type: _____ Age: _____ (approx.)
☐ Other:_____

Are there, to the best of your (Seller's) knowledge, any of the above that are not in operating condition? ☐ Yes ☐ No If yes, then describe. (Attach additional sheets if necessary.): _____

_____

_____

B. Are you (Seller) aware of any significant defects/malfunctions in any of the following? ☐ Yes ☐ No If yes, check **appropriate space(s) below.**
☐ Interior Walls ☐ Ceilings ☐ Floors ☐ Exterior Walls ☐ Insulation ☐ Roof(s) ☐ Windows ☐ Doors ☐ Foundation ☐ Slab(s)
☐ Driveways ☐ Sidewalks ☐ Walls/Fences ☐ Electrical Systems ☐ Plumbing/Sewers/Septics ☐ Other Structural Components
(Describe: _____

_____

_____)

If any of the above is checked, explain. (Attach additional sheets if necessary.): _____

_____

_____

Buyer and Seller acknowledge receipt of a copy of this page, which constitutes Page 1 of 2 Pages.
Buyer's Initials (_____) (_____) Seller's Initials (_____) (_____)

BROKER'S COPY

┌─── OFFICE USE ONLY ───┐
Reviewed by Broker or Designee _____
Date _____

EQUAL HOUSING OPPORTUNITY
SF-Jan-88

REAL ESTATE TRANSFER DISCLOSURE STATEMENT (TDS-14 PAGE 1 OF 2)

Subject Property Address _____

C. Are you (Seller) aware of any of the following:

1. Features of the property shared in common with adjoining landowners, such as walls, fences, and driveways. whose use or responsibility for maintenance may have an effect on the subject property. .... ☐ Yes ☐ No
2. Any encroachments, easements or similar matters that may affect your interest in the subject property. .... ☐ Yes ☐ No
3. Room additions, structural modifications, or other alterations or repairs made without necessary permits. .... ☐ Yes ☐ No
4. Room additions, structural modifications, or other alterations or repairs not in compliance with building codes. ...... ☐ Yes ☐ No
5. Landfill (compacted or otherwise) on the property or any portion thereof. .... ☐ Yes ☐ No
6. Any settling from any cause, or slippage, sliding, or other soil problems. .... ☐ Yes ☐ No
7. Flooding, drainage or grading problems. .... ☐ Yes ☐ No
8. Major damage to the property or any of the structures from fire, earthquake, floods, or landslides. .... ☐ Yes ☐ No
9. Any zoning violations, non-conforming uses, violations of "setback" requirements. .... ☐ Yes ☐ No
10. Neighborhood noise problems or other nuisances. .... ☐ Yes ☐ No
11. CC&R's or other deed restrictions or obligations. .... ☐ Yes ☐ No
12. Homeowners' Association which has any authority over the subject property. .... ☐ Yes ☐ No
13. Any "common area" (facilities such as pools, tennis courts, walkways, or other areas co-owned in undivided interest with others). .... ☐ Yes ☐ No
14. Any notices of abatement or citations against the property. .... ☐ Yes ☐ No
15. Any lawsuits against the seller threatening to or affecting this real property. .... ☐ Yes ☐ No

If the answer to any of these is yes, explain. (Attach additional sheets if necessary.): _____

_____

_____

_____

Seller certifies that the information herein is true and correct to the best of the Seller's knowledge as of the date signed by the Seller.

Seller _____ Date _____

Seller _____ Date _____

III
AGENT'S INSPECTION DISCLOSURE
(To be completed only if the seller is represented by an agent in this transaction.)
THE UNDERSIGNED, BASED ON THE ABOVE INQUIRY OF THE SELLER(S) AS TO THE CONDITION OF THE PROPERTY AND BASED ON A REASONABLY COMPETENT AND DILIGENT VISUAL INSPECTION OF THE ACCESSIBLE AREAS OF THE PROPERTY IN CONJUNCTION WITH THAT INQUIRY, STATES THE FOLLOWING:

_____

_____

_____

Agent (Broker
Representing Seller) _____ By _____ Date_____
                      (Please Print)   (Associate Licensee or Broker-Signature)

IV
AGENT'S INSPECTION DISCLOSURE
(To be completed only if the agent who has obtained the offer is other than the agent above.)
THE UNDERSIGNED, BASED ON A REASONABLY COMPETENT AND DILIGENT VISUAL INSPECTION OF THE ACCESSIBLE AREAS OF THE PROPERTY, STATES THE FOLLOWING:

_____

_____

_____

Agent (Broker
obtaining the Offer) _____ By _____ Date_____
                      (Please Print)   (Associate Licensee or Broker-Signature)

V
BUYER(S) AND SELLER(S) MAY WISH TO OBTAIN PROFESSIONAL ADVICE AND/OR INSPECTIONS OF THE PROPERTY AND TO PROVIDE FOR APPROPRIATE PROVISIONS IN A CONTRACT BETWEEN BUYER AND SELLER(S) WITH RESPECT TO ANY ADVICE/INSPECTIONS/DEFECTS.

I/WE ACKNOWLEDGE RECEIPT OF A COPY OF THIS STATEMENT.

Seller _____ Date_____ Buyer _____ Date_____

Seller _____ Date_____ Buyer _____ Date_____

Agent (Broker
Representing Seller) _____ By _____ Date_____
　　　　　　　　　　　(Please Print)　　　　　　　　　(Associate Licensee or Broker-Signature)

Agent (Broker
obtaining the Offer) _____ By _____ Date_____
　　　　　　　　　　　(Please Print)　　　　　　　　　(Associate Licensee or Broker-Signature)

A REAL ESTATE BROKER IS QUALIFIED TO ADVISE ON REAL ESTATE. IF YOU DESIRE LEGAL ADVICE, CONSULT YOUR ATTORNEY.

This form is available for use by the entire real estate industry.
The use of this form is not intended to identify the user as a
REALTOR®. REALTOR® is a registered collective membership
mark which may be used only by real estate licensees who are
members of the NATIONAL ASSOCIATION OF REALTORS®
and who subscribe to its Code of Ethics.

┌─── OFFICE USE ONLY ───┐
│ Reviewed by Broker or Designee _____ │
│ 　　　　　　Date _____ │
└──────────────────────┘

EQUAL HOUSING
OPPORTUNITY
SF-Jan-88

BROKER'S COPY

REAL ESTATE TRANSFER DISCLOSURE STATEMENT (TDS-14 PAGE 2 OF 2)

Follow-Up During Escrow

Check Complete

1. I will check with the title company to assess whether additional information is needed and whether there are any problems that will affect obtaining title. ☐

2. I will ensure that both you and your buyers receive copies of all documents pertinent to the transaction. I will have the buyer sign to acknowledge that he has received his copy. ☐

3. I will make sure that all contingencies are met and removed within the time limit provided or get an extension, if needed, signed by both you and the buyer. ☐

4. I will keep you abreast of the buyers' application for a loan and the progress of the appraisal on your home. ☐

5. I will cooperate with the appraiser to arrange for entry to the property and to answer any questions he may have about the home or neighborhood. I will also provide him with the most recent comparable sales in the area. ☐

6. I will make sure that the buyers' deposit is increased if required, as soon as the loan contingency is removed. ☐

7. I will coordinate all inspections and keep you informed of their findings. ☐
   a. Roof b. Pest Control c. Pool
   d. Building e. Buyers' walk through f. Etc.

8. I will cooperate with sellers and others involved to ensure that corrective work is completed according to the terms of the contract. ☐

9. I will ensure that all documents are ordered and drawn. ☐
   a. Pay-off b. Insurance for buyer

10. I will do my best to have your closing papers drawn one week before C.O.E. (Buyers also) so that if any problems arise, we can solve them and still keep you within the time frame that you expect. ☐

11. Whenever possible, I will hand-carry all documents as needed. ☐

12. I will coordinate the closing dates and move-in dates so that they are as convenient to both parties as possible. ☐

13. Prior to signing off, I will deliver a moving day checklist that you may use to coordinate your move. ☐

14. If you prefer, I will deliver your escrow check to you. ☐

Index